This Abund

InBetween
Living in the Tension Between Promise & Fulfillment

Mike Chong Perkinson
Tom Johnston

InBetween: Living in the Tension Between Promise and Fulfillment

www.praxismedia.org
Published by PraxisMedia, a ministry of
The Praxis Center for Church Development
PO Box 4878 Manchester, NH 03108

Cover design: Scott Greenlee

Interior design: Carol Brinson

ISBN: 978-0-9822727-0-1

Printed in the United States by Evangel Press

Contents

Foreword

I once heard the story told by an American missionary, working deep in the Amazon jungle. He was surprised one day to discover two young American tourists on their way through the jungle. The young travelers asked for some directions on their journey. The patient missionary did the best job possible to explain to these young tourists that in the jungle, one does not need directions or a map, what one really needs is a guide. A guide is one who knows the way and great dangers of the journey. The guide also knows the special delights and beauties along the pathway.

The book that you hold in your hands was written by two men who are experienced guides -- who know the way, the dangers, and the delights of Christian life -- and who share openly the mystery of this Christian journey.

Everybody has a story, and Mike and Tom, in their openness and transparency, boldly tell the story of what they have seen God do, as they have walked along the Christian pathway. Their unique experience of encounter with God and the story of His transformation, as they have discovered the way, will be a powerful challenge to every reader. Just as unique as every thumbprint, so the Christian adventure will be your unique story. No one else will ever have exactly the same story that you do. God is good; God is faithful, and He is still writing your story.

Don't miss the tremendous joy on this journey. God, Himself, is the center and source of all true joy. People love to talk about the things that they love. Those on this Christian journey have discovered that their joy in God is an experience that simply must be told to others along the way. "I am certain that God who began the good work within you, will continue His work until it is finally finished on the day when Christ Jesus returns." Philippians 1:6 NLT

Reverend Dr. David M. Midwood
President, Vision New England

Dedication & Acknowledgements

We would like to dedicate this book to Our Lord Jesus Christ, ruler of the Kingdom now and not yet - and over all of the land of in between.

To our wives...

From Mike - Teresa, I am grateful for the journey that we have had together as we have traveled through the land of in between, enjoying the hope that the promise brings and the love the Father has allowed us to share. Your faithful friendship and partnership in Christ has made life in between more radiant and alive. Thank you for loving me and always believing in me. As we journey towards the fulfillment, I am privileged to love you and be your husband and friend.

And to my two special daughters, Sierra and Asia, you have made my journey complete, providing me the tremendous honor of being your daddy. You make the in between a delight and joy and I love you as "big as God, Jesus, the Holy Spirit, the universe, the planets, the mountains, the volcanoes and infinity plus one."

From Tom - Cathy, in your journey through life, you have come to know what it means to have hope deferred, and yet you meet each circumstance with grace and determination, not willing to give in to a circumstance or situation. You are the model of perseverance, continuing to endure and press forward when most people would have given up. It is for this, and so much more, that I love you and am proud to be your husband. You are the perfect companion for an adventurer like me. Your faithfulness to the Lord stands as a testimony of who Jesus is in you. Thank you for walking together with me in this great adventure. I love you.

To our mentors...

We thank those people in our lives that have shaped us in Christ and helped us better understand the God of in between and live a life of faith and hope in the land of in between.

To Dr. Bob Logan - Thank you for setting us on this path we share together in this thing called Praxis. You have helped us start this journey and for that we will always be grateful and for your continued friendship and wise counsel. Thank you, oh wise Jedi Master. From your Jedi Knights, Obi-Wan and Obi-Chan (the Asian version).

Mike would like to thank Don Smith, Steve Overman and the late Dr. William L. Lane.

Don, thank you for being the purest example of Jesus I have had the privilege to be around. You are a man who has taught me how to live in the land of in between, always exemplifying faith, hope and love in every situation. Thank you, Don and Judy, for teaching me what it means to love God and love others and to have fun. Thanks for all the laughs and I expect many more. Don, you are a trusted friend and I deeply love and appreciate you.

Steve, you are a good friend and a man who has always provided me with solid counsel and direction. When I think of you, the word "steady" comes to mind, as you have with great faith navigated the waters of in between, finding ways to trust God and live on this planet as a faithful representative of the God of in between. Thank you Steve for your friendship - you are loved. Your friend, "Purgatory."

Dr. William L. Lane (Bill), I will forever be grateful for the investment you and your wife, Brenda, made in my life. Your belief in me and the encouraging way you were able to reinforce the gifting God placed in me helped transform my life and make me into the man I am today. Until I see you in heaven, Bill, know that I will honor your life by living out "Task Theology" in the land of in between. Your disciple until the promise of heaven is complete.

Tom would like to thank Ralph Moore, Dale Yancy and Jim Scott.

Ralph, thanks for cutting a trail that the rest of us could follow. It took hard work, endurance, a lot of perseverance and willingness to not compromise. I am grateful for both your work and for you as a man of God. I'm honored to be one of your spiritual offspring! Cathy and I love you and Ruby.

Dale, I just wanted to say "thank you" in a very public, written form for so many things: for infecting me with the church planter's virus; for giving me a shot at it when I was just a long haired kid working in a shoe store; for answering my endless stream of questions; and for caring for Cathy and me in the process. I continue to value your friendship and team work. We love you and Renée very much.

Sir James, I am grateful for your support and guidance, and for you being there at the dawn of Praxis. It was great to have your input during all those highly caffeinated sessions at Barnes & Nobles and Panera Bread. Your encouragement was instrumental in lighting the Praxis flame. Cathy and I love you, and Melinda and Mom, too! Wish you still lived on the "right" coast.

To our proofreaders...

Thanks to Dr. Eugene Luke, Donna Fry, Jodie McCay, Selina McGinnin, Catherine Maillet, Amy Jones, Bobbie Stifles, Kristin Caraway and Lorna Miller for wading through the pages of this book. You make us look good!

Those we live in community with...

Special thanks to the Harvest Community in New Hampshire, Estrella Mountain Church in Goodyear, Arizona. You make our lives rich with Jesus.

Special thanks to Carol Brinson for doing our page layout and to Scott Greenlee for the wonderful cover art – all green lights on a highway in the desert in the Land of InBetween (Isaiah 40:3).

Introduction to the Series

We come to this new series entitled This Abundant Life, with a great sense of anticipation. The name given to this series of books is rooted in a very well known scripture - John 10:10:

> *The thief comes only to steal and kill and destroy. I came that they may have life and have it abundantly.*

It is in this great statement, simple yet profound, brief but all-encompassing, that Jesus explains everything: how the sickness, pain, hurt, despair and death which we experience in this world are not acts of God, but acts of a thieving Enemy, and how Jesus has come to defeat that enemy and give us life -- life abundantly. It does not get more concise than that. There is no better explanation for the totality of our current human existence. We live in a world at war, amidst conflict between forces much larger than ourselves. One side wishes to destroy us. The other wishes to bless us with His life. Our main role in this conflict is simply to choose sides, and do so daily, even hourly.

The choice is about what to believe in the midst of a barrage of lies. We wage war continually upon the battlefields of our heart and our minds, choosing either lies or abundance, to believe the Destroyer or the Blessed One. In so choosing, we either become liberated, or sink deeper into the bonds of captivity.

Living in this war-torn environment of life, even for the Christian, is difficult and sometimes discouraging. Yet Jesus didn't come just so we could get by or muddle through. Rather He became a man, grew, lived, taught, was crucified, died, was buried and rose again so that we might have newness of life, and that life in abundance. Jesus didn't die so you could lose. He died that you might reign victoriously in this life and the next. However, He never promised a life without trouble or difficulty or conflict. Quite the opposite, being one of His disciples comes with all kinds of costs and will produce all kinds of conflicts and challenges. In the midst of all this, He promises life in abundance.

The abundant life which Jesus promises is not a life free from want, but it is a life free from wanting. It is a life of peace, contentment, inner comfort and joy by His Holy Spirit despite our circumstances, regardless of our situation. This life in Christ is abundant, and that abundance allows us contentment with godliness, which is great gain.

Our hope for you, our readers, is that through this series, Jesus may empower you to overcome your fear, insecurity and doubt and choose to live this abundant life daily.

May the Lord bless you as you as you embrace His abundance!
Mike Chong Perkinson
Tom Johnston

Introduction to the Book

Living life can be arduous and difficult. Well, at least we can say it is difficult to understand, especially when the goals or dreams or promises of God are no nearer now than they were years ago. Having one's dreams out of arm's reach is like being in the middle of a project or a book. There is something about the middle, the "in between" that sucks the motivation out of life. How many projects or books have been stopped half-way? How many lives stop half-way?

Life is that middle ground, that place where we live "in between" promise and fulfillment, since fulfillment rarely comes immediately, especially when it deals with God. How we live this life is the essence of our faith. Is our faith in the promise or the fulfillment? Or is our faith in the One who gives the promise? The in between of life answers the question for us and purifies our faith making us ever closer to the One who created us. It may not be a pleasant process, but it is a rewarding and life changing one that miraculously engages the heart to live life to the fullest in the power of the One who made us in His Image.

All Christians live a life in between promise and fulfillment. We live in the present with our eyes fixed on the future perfect Kingdom of God. Our hope in this book is to journey with you in this land of in between as we share our stories, hoping to better grasp this life of faith and trust as we make our way through it. We do not come as experts in this enterprise but as fellow sojourners, humbled, convicted and broken by the mystery of life and the love of a God who has been quick to forgive, steadfast in His presence and promise, and slightly slow in his deliverance as He seems to plod along at "three miles an hour." We are not saying God does not arrive or that His promises are null and void. What God promises will come to pass. We are acknowledging the reality you have already encountered many times -- that God's promises do come, but generally not in the timeframe you were hoping for.

Life is too short to spend it hiding, afraid, complaining, angry, etc. God is beyond our understanding and trying to figure Him out is futile. It does little for our faith but allow us to reduce God to a manageable deity that can better be controlled. No matter how many explanations we have, they do little to convince the mind or resolve the issue(s) of life, delay of promise, pain and suffering.

Life is best lived and best done on God's terms, living out participating in His Story centered in Jesus, the "yes" and "amen" of God. God has a promise for us all, and He longs to see it fulfilled in us; perhaps moving at "three miles an hour," moving nonetheless with a plan and purpose to make our lives something more than we can imagine. We pray you taste that in the in between of life, and may we all one day feast together in the ultimate fulfillment of life with God and each other, where promise will no longer be needed and fulfillment will be a present, eternal, reality.

May the words of this book bring you hope and help foster a closer relationship with the God of the universe, the fulfillment of all our promises. May you find His love more delightful and His process more pleasant as you enjoy Him as the fulfillment of life in between. He is the key after all -- the fulfillment of all our promises, "The one that will give you all you need from day to day if you live for Him and make the Kingdom of God your primary concern" (Matthew 6:33 NLT).

May you find all you need.

Mike Chong Perkinson
Tom Johnston

SECTION ONE

Promise & Delay

But do not overlook this one fact, beloved, that with the Lord one day is as a thousand years, and a thousand years as one day. The Lord is not slow to fulfill his promise as some count slowness, but is patient toward you, not wishing that any should perish, but that all should reach repentance. (2 Peter 3:8-9)

The thief comes only to steal and kill and destroy. I came that they may have life and have it abundantly. (John 10:10)

CHAPTER ONE

The Excitement of Promise: "Hope Embraced"

Mike was 13 years old when his mother had what she believed to be a dream from God. It was during a time when his father was living with another woman and rarely involved in the life of the family. This lapse in familial matters did not take away Mike's burning desire to see his father return to his mother as a man who had come to know the Savior. Mike along with his brother and mother prayed incessantly and believed in God for the miraculous. Then in one awesome dream they found their hearts stirred with hope and expectancy. God had revealed to Mike's mother that his father would one day be saved, living as a man of God, a faithful husband, and a father.

It was a jubilant morning when Mike's mother shared the news with her children about the awesome and overpowering dream she had about their father's future salvation. They could not help but have their faith rekindled and hearts swept away with hope. With the news of this dream, the posture of the family quickly changed from sadness to faithful and expectant seeking. They began to look for signs that their father was changing and waited diligently for the fulfillment to come. There was something about the promise that made each day alive and the hope of its fulfillment ravaged their souls with joyful enthusiasm.

There is nothing more delightful than hearing a word of hope or promise in the midst of what is sometimes a rather painful and mediocre life. The pleasant interruption by a word of hope into our world of constant responsibility and despair is a welcome intruder. It reshapes our world and invites us to believe and live again. The drive to find that place of rest and release burns in all who live on this planet, whether they are "in Christ" or not. It is precisely this drive that is awakened with fervor when a word of promise is given. We embrace the hope such words bring us, making them part of our reality.

We live in a world of promises. The promises of the customer service agent who ensures you the company will take care of your problem. The sales clerk who says that returns are no problem if you are not satisfied with your purchase; pastors that say the church is there to serve and be there to help in time of need; and the pastor who promises that living for Christ will result in a life of constant blessing. There is nothing like the hope of a promise that takes the blandness of a wish and graciously applies color to it. It can quickly transform the heart from the state of sadness to that of expectancy. Hope is a necessary ingredient in the matrix of life and the element of promise is the great fuel that allows hope to burn.

The anticipation of the fulfillment of such promises permits us to live life with wondrous expectancy. Like the child who knows that Christmas is near, the promise of gifts translates into eager expectation as he waits for that day to dawn. Promises give us something specific to look forward to, and maybe, something to live for. It's like having two slices of bread as one creates their favorite sandwich.

Life As A Sandwich

In the delightful movie, *Forrest Gump*, Forrest gave the world his simple wisdom when he said, "Life is like a box of chocolates. You never know what you are going to get." The joyful and positive approach to life that Forrest lived with provided him with a sense of surprise at every turn. In the same way, the wonderful world of promise moves us from the element of general surprise to hopeful expectation that something good is on the horizon.

But when dealing with promise and hope, we begin to see that life is like a sandwich. One slice of bread is the promise given, the other slice the promise received. Whatever one places in between the two slices of bread is the time of waiting for the promise to come to pass - the in between of life. Most of our lives are spent between the two slices of bread: promise and fulfillment.

When Mike met the Savior as a teen-age boy of 13, he was awestruck by the love and peace Christ gave him. Suddenly, a young boy without his earthly father's attention, he found himself in a new world of acceptance, forgiveness, and hope. What was once lost and confusing became alive. His world of impossibilities was transformed into a world of possibilities and faith. In one eternal moment he found himself comforted with the awesome awareness that God would take care of his life. It was then that he learned that Jesus wanted Mike's heavy yoke in exchange for His easy yoke.

As Mike grew in the things of the Lord, yet found life wanting, it became increasingly difficult for him to understand the vagaries of life and the delay of the promise. It felt like he was sandwiched in the middle of something with no way out. But he discovered that somewhere between one slice and the other is this thing we call life. That is, as Christians we live between two slices of bread. One slice is the slice of promise and the other of fulfillment. If we look to our ancient past in the Old Testament, we see that our Christian existence is like living between the promise of deliverance from Egypt and the fulfillment of the promised land in Canaan (Exodus 3:16-17). The promise gives us hope that we will one day obtain the great blessing of life in full with Jesus, the Promised Land. But for now, we live in between and wait, and the waiting makes embracing words of hope and promise so very difficult. There is nothing that seems to squelch the life of a promise more than delay.

Tom's life, strikingly similar to Mike's in their early environment and upbringing, also has a unique element of living in between. Diagnosed at age 33 with Cystic Fibrosis, Tom is in the position of living with a condition that kills most of those afflicted by the age of 25. Tom is now 44, and has a team of physicians and medical specialists who care for him. While the Cystic Fibrosis has not killed him, it often impairs his normal function in life and ministry. This genetic disorder has prevented him from having children of his own. Although his own healing has not manifested, Tom has found that the people he prays for are healed by Jesus Christ on a regular basis; he is used by the Lord to bring wholeness to others. While looking forward to his own healing, which is not yet manifested, he is used by the Lord to bring wholeness to others. In addition, while he cannot have natural children, the Lord has used him to "give birth" to churches, pastors and Christian leaders widely. He lives in between, used by the Lord to fulfill His promises to others, while not yet having received himself the fullness of what the Lord has for him.

The Life of Joseph

If there is anyone who was familiar with the in between, I dare say it was Joseph. The life of Joseph powerfully portrays for us how life is to be lived as a sandwich. In the book of Genesis, we meet Joseph as an arrogant and spoiled 17 year-old who has dreams (from God) of his brothers falling down before him as a ruler (27:1-11). However, it is not until Joseph is 39 years old (45:11, "there are yet five years of famine to come", meaning the seven years of abundance were over, see Genesis 41:46-49 - add nine years to 30, for 39) that his brothers actually bow before him as in his youthful dream. It's hard to believe that 22 years of Joseph's life have been spent dealing with rejection (37:18-20), lies (37:26-35; 39:6-18), prison (39:19-20), and being forgotten (40:23) since the promise was given. The story of Joseph makes it very clear that God's promise will always be fulfilled but not necessarily in the time frame we so often desire.

The reality of fallen nature is not something new. Dysfunction and weirdness have been part of human life since the Fall of Adam and Eve. In fact, the stories of the Old Testament tell of events such as we have noted in the life of Joseph. This is one of the many elements that endear us to the Bible: It presents its characters and heroes in all their human frailties. For example, the narrative is very clear in Genesis 37:3 that Jacob loved Joseph more than the other children. What makes this statement so poignant is that Jacob demonstrates this favor by giving Joseph a special robe of many colors. This was to set him apart and give him regal status. Jacob favored Joseph over his brothers, setting the stage for jealousy, envy, gossip, distrust, and even hatred amongst them.

In spite of this, the story drives home the point of sovereignty, as it explains how God moves in the painful moments of life and how he uses negative situations to manifest His will and purpose. The dreams Joseph has as a young man of 17 (Genesis 37:1-11) are not actualized until he has gone through severe pain and trials, living in the reality of in between. By the time the dreams come to partial fulfillment, he is 30 years old (41:46). Thirteen years go by for a young man who has been nearly murdered and rejected by his brothers, falsely accused of rape by his employer's wife and sent to jail.

What makes the story line so dramatic is the negative turn of events Joseph encounters right after he has the youthful dreams. It is as if the promise is the instigator of Joseph's demise. No matter which way he turns, tragedy of some sort awaits him. Maybe the greatest blow to his young heart is his own family, his brothers in particular, turning against him. The threefold refrain, "they hated him," (37:4, 5, 8) reverberates in our passage culminating in Genesis 37:11: "his brothers were jealous of him." The familial tension and dysfunction sets the stage for the whole story, a story that sounds incredibly familiar to a life many lead today.

It appears the story of Joseph is all about promise and fulfillment in the in between of life. For it is the story of a spoiled child and a dreamer, sold into slavery by his jealous brothers, subjected to various trials, and culminating in his becoming a ruler (second only to Pharaoh). Joseph is divinely placed as a ruler in Egypt (mysteriously placed in every situation) by God to save his people and countless others in dire need from famine.

Before we go any further, we must understand the connection the story has with the history of the patriarchs, Abraham, Isaac, and Jacob. After all, the story line of Joseph (micro-story) is a fulfillment of the promise given to Abraham (the larger or macro-story) about being a great nation (Genesis 12:2). The promise to Abraham is seriously challenged by the famine and the move to Egypt by Joseph's father, Jacob, and his family. Here we see that the promise is not forgotten, for the Lord speaks to Jacob and reassures him in Genesis 46:3-4. "Do not be afraid to go down to Egypt, for I will see to it that you become a great nation there. I will go with you down to Egypt, and I will bring your descendents back again" (NLT). It is precisely because moving to Egypt appears to place the fulfillment of the promise in jeopardy that Jacob needs to be reassured that God will be with him there and that he will return. Our story explains how Jacob went from living in Canaan to settling in Egypt. This is no mere accident or result of human nature, but an act of God's sovereign will, a reassuring word that the Spirit of God often gives us in the midst of those seasons where it would appear that what God has promised won't transpire. And so, as the Joseph story is finding its fulfillment, God is also working fulfillment for the family of Abraham, Isaac, and Jacob as He so powerfully preserves the family through the great famine. There are more promises and fulfillments at play in our human enterprise than we could ever imagine. The great chess game of life has so many masterful and critical moves that God, as the Grandmaster Himself, carefully and lovingly provides us the necessary ingredients for life in between as the promise weaves its way into fulfillment in our lives.

We find in our own larger (macro) stories that when we come to Christ there is a delightful sense of life that is experienced and hope that is renewed. Our hearts are awakened and our spirits made alive as we come to understand the nature and purpose of our existence. Salvation delivers us from the oppressive bondage of life and releases us to hope and life that is in Christ. The slice of bread, called salvation, wonderfully gives us hope for the future, heaven, and all that awaits us, the second slice. Having these two slices of bread gives us perspective and helps us live in between as we deal with the micro-stories of our lives, our promises of healing, blessing, the promised job, career, mate, etc.

The book of Genesis closes with the promise on the lips of the patriarchs, but it is a promise that is still far from being fulfilled. It is clear that Genesis needs a sequel. The promise is not yet complete. And so, with Joseph and his family we wait.

What Promise Is

In our world a promise can be described as a breath of fresh air, a cool breeze on a hot day. There is something about its presence that restores the soul and lifts the heart to new measures of possibility and life. As we embrace promise we find ourselves embraced by a new stance and posture on life which enables us to live with passion. Promise is the prelude to hope. It is that word that generates life and hope in our spirits. It moves us to live and embrace life with vitality. Without promise there is no hope, and without hope words of promise are meaningless.

When we turn our gaze from the modern world and look to the Old Testament, we will not find a specific word for promise. Where our English translations say that someone promised something, the Hebrew simply states that someone said or spoke some word with a future reference. More specifically, a promise is a word that goes forth into time. It reaches ahead of its speaker and its recipient, to mark an appointment between them and the future. A promise may be an assurance of continuing or future action on behalf of someone: "I will be with you;" "They that mourn will be comforted;" "If we confess our sins, he is faithful and just, and will forgive our sins." Promise can also function in the arena of covenant language where a solemn agreement of lasting and mutual, even if unequal, relationship is struck. It can also function as an announcement of a future event: "When you have brought the people from Egypt, you will serve God on this mountain." It is of great interest that when we find an oath it is often accompanied by a word of promise (Exodus 6:8; Deuteronomy 9:5; Hebrews 6:13).

The language of promise makes it clear that what God has spoken with His mouth will be performed by His hand. One can say that such promises from Him are signposts of a future hope, for His word does not return void. "God is not man, that he should lie, or a son of man, that he should change his mind. Has he said, and will he not do it? Or has he spoken, and will he not fulfill it?" (Numbers 23:19) If God speaks it, then it is as good as done. The New Testament takes this thought in regards to our salvation and provides the picture of earnest money or a down payment as the guarantee that what God began He will finish in us (Ephesians 1:14; Philippians 1:6). Unlike human beings and heathen gods, God knows and commands the future (1 Kings 8:15, 24, Isaiah 41:4, 26; 43:12, 19, etc.; Romans 4:21). This is precisely what brings the human heart hope. The solid conviction that God is actually running our universe, expressing His will, as He reveals His love and life to His creation through His Son, Jesus Christ, is the very thing that comforts our distressed hearts even in the in between.

The Content of the Promise: Grace, Mercy, and Forgiveness

The sequel or point of convergence of the Old Testament promises to Abraham, Moses, David and the Fathers through the prophets is Jesus Christ. Jesus is the "Yes" of God and through Him all the promises of God are fulfilled and affirmed by the church in the "Amen" of its worship (2 Corinthians 1:19-20). The promised Word, the Logos (John 1:14), has become flesh. As the late Dr. William L. Lane said, "When God gives a gift; He wraps it in a person." The incarnation is the gift of presence, the unveiled hope that provides for us a living hope (1 Peter 1:3). This new covenant has been inaugurated upon the "better promises" (Hebrews 8:6-13) prophesied by the prophet Jeremiah (Jeremiah 31). Jesus is the guarantee (Hebrews 7:22), and as already noted, the Holy Spirit of promise is the first installment (Ephesians 1:13-14).

The good news we are called to live and profess is the radical truth that our God loves us and has provided the guarantee of His promise in and through Jesus. Ironically, this promise of grace and forgiveness from God is precisely the problem we often have with God. It's the problem of Jonah as he complains to God:

> ..."Didn't I say before I left home that you would do this, LORD? That is why I ran away to Tarshish! I knew that you were a gracious and compassionate God, slow to get angry and filled with unfailing love. I knew how easily you could cancel your plans for destroying these people. Just kill me now, LORD! I'd rather be dead than alive because nothing I predicted is going to happen." (Jonah 4:2-3 NLT)

In other words, I knew you would forgive these pagans. Much like the crazy farmer in Matthew 20, God takes in people at the last hour and pays them the same amount as those who have worked the whole day. Something in us cries out that it is not fair. It's the reply of the older brother in the parable of the prodigal son in Luke 15 as he complains that the father has never done this for him. It appears that our God takes the issue of promise to a delightful extreme as He takes in freeloaders and unworthy people, pays off their debt, cleans them up, gives them a life and a family, and provides them with a future (Jeremiah 29:11; Colossians 2:13-15). Although our hearts cry out for mercy as we reach for the promise in our lives, there is something that screams for justice when the promise of grace and forgiveness is extended to those whom we deem late-comers or undeserving of such kindness. You know, those brothers of Joseph that tried to kill him and sold him into slavery, that man that molested you, the friend who took your lover. Need we go on?

The love of God is like a credit card company that tells you they will forgive your debt because someone has already paid it for you. Forgiveness can't be earned, it can only be granted. God loves us and there is nothing we can do to change that. As He says in the book of Isaiah, "Can a mother forget her nursing child? Can she feel no love for a child she has borne? But even if that were possible, I would not forget you!" (Isaiah 49:15). God's love is not a responsive love based on the response of the object loved. His love is the source. He acts. He does not react. He initiates love. This is what is known as unconditional love. In other words,

> ...God loves us like Beauty loved the Beast (the great fairy tale made into a Walt Disney classic). There was nothing beautiful about the Beast that caused Beauty to love him. Rather it was her love that made him beautiful. Unconditional love does not mean that God loves us and it does not matter what we do, rather it means that there is nothing in us that draws Him to us. Eros love is that love which is aroused when one sees beauty in another and loves the beauty within them. This is not to say such love is wrong, but to simply describe the love that is most familiar to humanity. Agape love, God's unconditional love, is the love that loves because God is love. In other words, God loves us not because we are beautiful - there is nothing in Him that needs anything. Rather He gives love to us and it is His love that makes us beautiful. And so, unconditional love is that love that is given to us by God that is based on Him and not us. Which means His love will never change because there was nothing we could to do to gain it and nothing we can do to lose it. (Johnston and Perkinson 19)

The sinner is then accepted even before he repents. Forgiveness is granted and he or she only needs to accept the gift. The Gospel of Jesus Christ is the love story of God with us. It begins with a radical forgiveness, the sole reality of the good news and the basis of the promise.

The story of Hosea captures the love of God quite profoundly as it depicts the heart of a broken God who loves an unfaithful bride. Hosea, representing God as the faithful and brokenhearted husband, is to marry a prostitute (Gomer), representing the unfaithful people of Israel (Hosea 1:2). Gomer won't refrain from having other lovers, carrying on to the point of bearing children that do not belong to Hosea (Hosea 1:9; 2:4-5). In spite of this unfaithfulness that drives an arrow of pain into the heart of her faithful husband, he loves her too much to divorce her. And so, God, the faithful and brokenhearted husband, makes a covenant with himself to make this relationship work (Hosea 2:14-23). In simple language, God's love for us is not based on us. It is based on Himself.

The picture from Hosea is quite graphic and painful to read as it describes God's bride as unfaithful, sleeping with other lovers. The language is poignant and indicts all of us as those who have flirted with the devil and ultimately have "slept" with him, violating our covenant relationship with God. This marital violation and anguish of God is clearly depicted in two verses in the book of Hosea as the prophet writes:

> She doesn't realize that it was I who gave her everything she has-the grain, the wine, the olive oil. Even the gold and silver she used in worshiping the god Baal were gifts from me! (Hosea 2:8 NLT)

> Oh, how can I give you up, Israel? How can I let you go? How can I destroy you like Admah and Zeboiim? My heart is torn within me, and my compassion overflows. No, I will not punish you as much as my burning anger tells me to. I will not completely destroy Israel, for I am God and not a mere mortal. I am the Holy One living among you, and I will not come to destroy. (Hosea 11:8-9 NLT)

The bleeding heart of God is most graphically described here as the prophet Hosea portrays God as almost human; indecisive and unsure of what He is going to do with His unfaithful bride. It's almost as if God, in a moment of eternity, didn't know what to do. We realize the tension of such a statement and we do not make it to challenge the all knowing nature of God, but to simply reinforce how deep His love is for us. In spite of the fact that we have fornicated with the devil, believed that it was our lovers, not God, who provided for us, He still humbles Himself by becoming one of us (John 1:14) and is obedient to the point of death on a cross so that our relationship with Him can be restored (Philippians 2:5-11).

Let's see if we can take all this theology and bring it into our human framework. Mike's daughter received a fish for her fifth birthday, a cute and delightful, although somewhat risky present for a little girl to have and enjoy. The goldfish lasted a few short hours before Mike's little girl, overcome with curiosity, reached in and grabbed the little fish and took it out of its environment. She was not trying to be cruel to the fish but desired to simply hold it and give it some love. Loving a fish with human touch and affection can be rather detrimental to the fish. The poor little fish never survived this as it died some 12 hours later. There was no way for Mike's little girl to communicate to the fish that she was trying to love it. Mike's daughter could show love and care for the fish in many ways, feeding it, cleaning the water, and coming around and talking to the fish daily, but she could not hold it or demonstrate affection.

What struck Mike about this is that no matter how hard one tried to communicate with the fish, it would always misunderstand what you were trying to do. The fragile little goldfish could only experience the benefits of love but not fully understand why this large being (Mike's daughter) was hanging around in its reality. The only way for this fish to grasp the love of Mike's daughter would be for her to become a little fish, speak fish, and show the little fish just how much she loved it. Oh how God must love us to undergo such extreme measures in restoring such unfaithful fish.

To help us understand this more, we turn to Frederick Buechner, who uses the Greek word, "agape," for God's love and the Greek word, "eros," for human love. He then goes on to describe God's love in this way:

> Agape does not want. It gives. It is not empty. It is full to overflowing. Paul strains to get the distinction right. Agape is patient: eros chomps at the bit. Agape puts up with anything; eros insists on having things its own way. Agape is kind-never jealous, boastful, rude. It does not love because but simply loves-the way rain falls or the sun shines. It 'bears all things,' up to and including even its own crucifixion. And it has extraordinary power. (Buechner, *The Clown in the Belfry* 56-57)

The Bible makes it clear that "we love because he first loved us" (1 John 4:19). God's unconditional love is then based on Himself and not us. God, much like a proud parent, loves the image of Himself in us. It is as if He said on that glorious sixth day of creation, "Look, Adam has your nose. Look how he smiles like you, Father."

Paul makes it clear that we are "rooted and grounded in love" (Ephesians 3:17). More simply, love is the soil in which believers are to be planted and grow, the foundation on which they are built. This foundation of love is not something that is experienced alone, but with another you "may have strength to comprehend with all the saints what is the breadth and length and height and depth" (Ephesians 3:18). Grasping the love of God is then something we do with the whole church, with all the saints.

Experiencing the content of promise is not something we do alone, but with those who are part of the greater family of God, the Church.

One of the great promises of Scripture is the return of Christ. There have been thousands of trees that have given of themselves to fill pages of books with various views and interpretations as to when Christ will return, and this is a major element of living in between - looking for His appearing. We echo the words of Pastor Jack Hayford who has said, "We are in the last days, the last of the last days." We do believe in Christ's literal and bodily return but are not all that sure as to the exact date. There is a passage that indicates that no one will know the time (Matthew 24:36) and so, we do not even pretend to know. What we simply wish to state is that Christ is coming and it is a promise that brings us hope of a day that will finally usher in God's Kingdom reign in full, restoring creation fully, righting all the wrongs of our human condition, and giving the devil a one way ticket to a special place created just for him.

As the Church awaits the promise of Christ's coming and of the new heavens and a new earth (2 Peter 3:4, 9, 13), it does not do so passively. Rather, the body of Christ sets forth on her missionary task of making disciples with the full assurance of God's presence (Matthew 28:20) and with the good news that the promise of the Father, the Holy Spirit (given to us as indicated in Joel 2:28), is given to everyone in Jesus Christ, fulfilling the promise to Abraham of universal blessing through his posterity. As we await the return of Christ, God is in the process of fulfilling many promises, both small and large. The "Alpha and the Omega" will one day come and bring to pass all that was promised. You hope not in vain. The promise is connected to faith and open to all, who by having faith as Abraham did, become children of the promise (Galatians 3).

The content of the Biblical promise is fulfilled and finalized in Jesus. Promise is about restoration which involves salvation as inheritance, life, Spirit, righteousness, and discovering and living out one's life as sons and daughters of the King (Romans 4:13; Galatians 3:14; Romans 9:8; Ephesians 1:13). One can say that Christ's loving act of sacrifice restores us to our place of royalty. After all, sons and daughters of a King are better known as princes and princesses. It was C. S. Lewis who reminded us that if we could see the real nature of people, we would fall at their feet in worship for the beauty or fear they would emanate (Martindale and Root 246). Like Beauty loving the Beast and restoring him to his original state of being a prince, this is precisely what the saving work of Christ does for fallen princes and princesses who really do not know who they are or who their Father really is. It is a truth the devil would not like us to ever discover.

Let us summarize this a little more formally. All the promises are fulfilled in Christ as the Yes of God (2 Corinthians 1:20) who took the curse of the law (Galatians 3:13) and gave the Spirit as a pledge, deposit, or seal (Ephesians 1:13-14). Mike has a friend who oversees the international missions department of a major denomination. When Mike meets with this key leader, he often tells him that whatever he wants to do, the answer is yes. What this bright and gifted leader is saying is that he believes in Mike and wants to find a way to assure that whatever Mike is proposing gets accomplished somehow. What he is not saying is that whatever Mike wants to do, he will do. God does something incredibly similar as he tries to find a way to say yes to our lives. In Christ is that final and ultimate YES that paves the way for restoration and fullness of life. It's as if God is saying to you and me, "Whatever you want to do the answer is Yes/Jesus."

More simply, Christ paid the price for our wrongs (sins) and then provided the down payment with the person of the Holy Spirit as the guarantee that His intention to restore us fully is genuine. It would be like a wonderful benefactor coming along and paying off the debts of every human being, paying the price for every criminal offense, and making it possible for all to enjoy their new found life and freedom. All we would have to do is acknowledge this gift, confess how we were wrong, go to those we had wronged and make it right if at all possible, and receive the generous love of the benefactor. The catch to this great gift is that it must be picked up in person. What if this were all you had to do to receive the love and gift of such a generous person? It would be good news and that is exactly what the gospel of Jesus is, GOOD NEWS. If you have not made that call to God yet, you might want to pause at this point and talk to the Great Benefactor, your Heavenly Father, and ask Him to save you from the debt you have incurred in this life.

> The great promise of the Scripture, our Promised Land if you will, is that:
>
> [But] Christ has rescued us from the curse pronounced by the law. When he was hung on the cross, he took upon himself the curse for our wrongdoing. For it is written in the Scriptures, "Cursed is everyone who is hung on a tree." Through the work of Christ Jesus, God has blessed the Gentiles with the same blessing he promised to Abraham, and we Christians receive the promised Holy Spirit through faith. (Galatians 3:13-14 NLT)

The content of the promise is then the gift of God in Jesus who came

> ...to take the punishment for our sins and to satisfy God's anger against us. We are made right with God when we believe that Jesus shed his blood, sacrificing his life for us. God was being entirely fair and just when he did not punish those who sinned in former times. And he is entirely fair and just in this present time when he declares sinners to be right in his sight because they believe in Jesus. (Romans 3:25-26 NLT)

A life of freedom awaits you and can only come by believing in the promise that was most radically demonstrated by the life, death, and resurrection of the great Yes of God, His Son, Jesus.

The Kingdom "Now" and "Not Yet"

Like Joseph in the Old Testament, Christians today live life in the in between of God's Kingdom. We live in between the first and second coming of the Lord Jesus Christ. We have all the blessing of his kingdom's rule and reign, but not yet in their fullness. Even our great attempts at proclaiming healing of the body are only temporary measures. The grand miracles of healing that still take place worldwide are, at best, temporary healings because we still die. We experience the Kingdom now and not yet. There will be a day when we are permanently healed in body, soul and spirit the completion of His dominion, looking for the day when Revelation 21:3-5 comes to pass:

> And I heard a loud voice from the throne saying, "Now the dwelling of God is with men, and he will live with them. They will be his people, and God himself will be with them and be their God. He will wipe every tear from their eyes. There will be no more death or mourning or crying or pain, for the old order of things has passed away." (NIV)

More simply said, there will no longer be any in between. However, we live in the Kingdom of God now, looking for the completion of the Kingdom that is not yet here. We live in between as sojourners looking for a better country. And yet, we can still partake of the goodness of His grace in salvation, healing, restoration and personal transformation. The Kingdom of

God in the now is not all encompassing, but is primarily internal to the human heart, or "righteousness and peace and joy in the Holy Spirit" (Romans 14:17b). We have been given the Holy Spirit as a deposit or guarantee of our future inheritance in Christ while awaiting the fullness of God's promised Kingdom yet to come. (Ephesians 1:13-14).

Therefore, living in the now of the Kingdom will require us to constantly address and embrace the tension of living in between the promise and future fullness, the now and the not yet of the Kingdom of God. And just like Joseph, who had no idea of how good his future would be, we do not have the slightest imaginings of how wonderful eternity with our God will be!

CHAPTER TWO

The Delay of Promise: "Hope Deferred"

Being interrupted in the middle of something can be deflating to one's motivation for completing the task at hand. Interruption somehow moves the purposed intent from passion to demise. Somehow we lose our way, our focus, and our purpose when we are half way or in the middle. Likewise, being stuck in between the now and not yet of the Kingdom of God can cause us to lose focus, and having lost that, we lose our motivation.

There is an obvious tension in this life. We find ourselves living lives that seek out solutions for and control of the dilemma of humanness. In other words, we do all that we possibly can to control the mystery of life. If you are someone who has been crushed by a broken promise, the alternative to such disappointment and despair is living a life of control. Of course, all control is really an illusion, but nonetheless we still try to control our lives. The sad fact is that once we opt for lives of control we end up destroying the mystery of life, and we are left with only empty areas of the soul that need filling. The precise result of a life of control is predictability, and predictability finds its full expression in boredom. Maybe this is why we are so bored.

The simple solution to our lives can be illustrated grammatically; we very often live either in the active or passive voice. That is, to solve the dilemma of life we either actively control our lives (active voice, the control posture) or we passively let others dictate our lives (passive voice, the victim posture).

Both reactions to the complexity of life resolve the immediate tension we feel. After all, how do we find identity in a world that makes little sense? We pray and nothing happens. We don't pray and someone is healed. Or like

Tom, we pray for others to be healed and they are while Tom waits for his own personal healing. We live in righteousness and life falls apart. We live in self-absorbed bitterness and greed and life is blessed. It is easy to understand why people opt to take control of their lives. After all, if no one else will watch out for good ole' number one, we might as well do it. This dilemma even explains why people opt for the passive role of victim. After all, if they can't control anything anyway, they are but pawns in the massive chess game of life, echoing the words of the character Eeyore, from *Winnie the Pooh*, "Why bother?"

However, there is another option that is not regularly considered. If we live most of our lives in between then we had best learn how to live in the middle. That is, we need to learn how to live life in the middle voice. In order for us to grasp a sense of who we are, we must first come to realize which voice we are to live in. We do not control the action. The pagan or secular concept of religion is that we pray and move the gods so they might act according to our agenda. I am not in control of the action nor am I controlled by the action is a Hindu concept of religion that affords one permission to sit passively by as the gods or fate exercise their desires. While we wait in an incomplete Kingdom awaiting its fullness, we are definitely NOT in control. We wait on a King to complete His work and bring the Kingdom in its completeness. The King is the ONLY one who is in control. As Tom is known to say, "All control is an illusion."

Living life in the middle voice is learning to accept the mystery of life. It is realizing that the King is moving in our world and we have the privilege of participating in the results, having a part in making history, His Story. It is the mystery that His will is fully engaged in the process of life along with mine. To somehow explain this to our satisfaction destroys the element of faith and vibrancy of life that is meant to be experienced in this mystery we call life.

Let us say a little more on His Story. We are all participants in God's world, His Story. This is not to say that God is the grand master and we are pawns in a divine chess game, being moved at will by the powers that be. Rather, it is a way to say that life is larger than us and really not about us. It is then not so much how we make our own history that matters, but how we allow ourselves to be willing participants in His Story. The issue we struggle with is how to incorporate God into our lives, find ways that we can add Him to our existence, letting God ride in the back seat while we drive, to learn the right steps and processes so that we can somehow manage and control our life in God, or to simply give up to the Great Master of the Universe and live passively, resigned to accepting that it doesn't matter what we do because God is going to do what he wants anyway. Whether we want to realize it or not, we are not the centerpiece of His Story. He is. His Story does not revolve around us; we are simply caught up in it. His Story is about restoring His unquestioned rule in the Earth, which has an intentional byproduct - the salvation of humankind. This is even more frustrating to the human heart. Not only are we not in control, but the grand epic metanarrative of life does not have us at the center! Living in between the beginning and end of this restoration story is what creates the tension for us caught in this middle time of the Kingdom.

Living life in the middle can only be fulfilling if centered in His Story (Christ) and lived in the middle voice, participating with God in His Story. However, being caught between the reality of promise and fulfillment fosters a restlessness and anxiety too common to life. If it appears that the promise is going to be delayed, then motivation can suffer all the more. We see this dilemma in 2 Peter 3:4 as it describes scoffers in the last days whom play on the delay of the return of Christ. "Where is the promise of his coming? For ever since the fathers fell asleep, all things are continuing as they were from the beginning of creation." The apostle then must not only remind the hearers that "The Lord is not slack concerning His promise, as some count slackness," but also finds it critical to explain why the delay is taking place as He notes that God "is longsuffering toward us, not willing that any should perish but that all should come to repentance" (2 Peter 3:9 NKJV).

Now if we factor in any of life's difficult moments, like having parents or friends who have promised the world and failed to deliver, then we find that "Hope deferred makes the heart sick" (Proverbs 13:12a NKJV). There is nothing more detrimental to the heart's ability to hope than having a promise given and not acted upon. As promises fail in our lives or delay in their fulfillment, we find it increasingly more difficult to muster up any hope or motivation to believe. It is difficult to think happy thoughts and fly to Neverland when failed promises have clipped our wings of hope. It is simply hard to continue to hope when the delay is long. There has to be something within or without that moves us to believe and hope again. Otherwise the inevitable occurs; the heart grows sick and tired. It recoils into the land of dispassionate living and its passion dies.

Many live their lives anticipating the worst. It is as if the faith mechanism has reversed, due to negativity and lack of fulfilled promises. Helen Hayes, the actress, exhibits this kind of living for us. She tells the following story in her autobiography. It was Thanksgiving Day, and she was cooking her first turkey dinner for her family. Before serving it she announced to her husband, Charles MacArthur, and their son James: "Now I know this is the first turkey I've ever cooked. If it isn't any good, I don't want anybody to say a word. We'll just get up from the table, without comment, and go out to a restaurant to eat." Then she returned to the kitchen. When she entered the dining room bearing the turkey, she found her husband and son seated at the table with their hats and coats on (quoted in Krieg 1.)

Many are living life with their hats and coats on, preparing for the worst. Murphy's Law says that if anything can go wrong, it will. Anticipating the worst or not hoping for the best is no way to live and yet, many live with little or no hope or anticipation of fulfillment. We are ever so painfully aware that living in between is difficult.

Delay: The Essence of Life

Trying to understand the seasons of life is difficult. Finding sanity in a fast-paced world moving without concern for your ability to keep up is frustrating. Many Christians attempt to find the life Jesus promised but come up short. The stories of victory only intensify our frustration and increase the volume of the question: "So, why am I not experiencing this in my life?" "How long must I wait until I find the fulfillment Jesus promised?" Even Jesus' original disciples lived in this tension, as they asked Him just before His ascension,

> So when they met together, they asked him, "Lord, are you at this time going to restore the kingdom to Israel?"
>
> He said to them: "It is not for you to know the times or dates the Father has set by his own authority. But you will receive power when the Holy Spirit comes on you; and you will be my witnesses in Jerusalem, and in all Judea and Samaria, and to the ends of the earth." (Acts 1:6-8 NIV)

These men had just spent three years with Jesus, seen His death, experienced His resurrection, and they still don't get it. And Jesus doesn't even answer their question! He says, "Never mind about that right now." He doesn't give them the answer, He doesn't promise the fulfillment of His Kingdom rule. All He does is promise the empowerment to live effectively for Him as witnesses. What He promised them, the coming of the Holy Spirit, was awesome, but as U2 says in one of their classic songs, they still hadn't found what they were looking for. Their hope and expectation in regards to the immediate coming of the Kingdom is left unfulfilled.

Realistically, more Christians live in the land of unfulfilled faith than do those who experience life to the full. Maybe this is why so many followers of Christ settle for a life of mediocrity. As boring and predictable as mediocrity is, it does allow one to handle the abrupt pain of disappointment and disillusionment. This is not the scenario God intended. Just like Jesus' disciples on the Mount of Ascension, our focus on the thing we want now causes us to miss the really big thing God wishes to do in us, and through us. We settle for mediocrity, life at the middle, rather than believe Him for great things. This results in the church offering over-simplified answers and solutions, only to compound the pain. For example, many have been told by fellow Christians that the reason they are not healed is because they do not have enough faith. The condemnation and despair is only heightened in the midst of such insensitive remarks. By "insensitive" we do not mean to imply the person did not mean well, but to suggest the perplexity of life is not viewed in full perspective by many. Nor are we implying that faith is not necessary for God to act as there are countless examples of such in the Scripture.

There is a dire need within the community of the faithful for a strong dose of reality. The temptation to pretend all is well and hold on to some form of bleak promise is all too common in our church world. Like Jesus' disciples in Acts 1, we figuratively stand looking blankly into the sky. But what else does one do when the delay of the promise is giving life to hopelessness and despair? God forbid that we should somehow honestly admit that we do not understand the timing and will of God. Until we allow ourselves to be stretched by the confusion of life we will not grasp the message of Scripture. For many churches and Christians the following is unfortunately true.

> The community of God's people is no place to deal with real concerns eating away at your lives; we exist to maintain orthodox belief and promote conforming behavior. Helping you with your personal problems is not the business of the church. (Crabb, *Understanding People* 52)

Regretfully, one of the results of being fallen creatures is our fear of truth. We tend to avoid responsibility for our own lives. By this, we mean people will take care of everything except that which really matters. Adam did not want to admit why he was naked in the garden. Instead of admitting to his sin, he carefully blamed the woman and ultimately, God. Our plight is the same. We struggle with what the real problem is and will do everything we can to find another explanation. We are in no way suggesting that life is not difficult and full of things that disturb us. What we are saying is that the source of our problems is not how life is, but what we are doing with it in relationship to God. We either choose to blame someone or something else and seek independence, or admit to our need to have life be the way we want without surrender to God. The issue for Adam is not just that he was naked and feeling shame, but that he had disobeyed God and would not admit it. It was not the woman who made him eat the fruit or God who was to blame because He made the woman. It was Adam's choice and the results of that choice impacted not only him but you and me.

It is easy to comprehend things you can control, but what do you do with things that you cannot control? Mike did not ask for a dad who would beat him and try to kill his mom, or to live with the reality of divorced parents. Tom did not ask to have Cystic Fibrosis, or to be childless. The list could go on and on. Our hearts scream for justice and constancy. Why doesn't life cooperate more? Why does every garden have to contain weeds? The Bible does not flinch in its candid expression of life. David writes, "When I weep and fast before the LORD, they scoff at me. When I dress in sackcloth to show sorrow, they make fun of me" (Psalm 69:10-11 NLT). He also writes:

> Their insults have broken my heart,
> and I am in despair.
> If only one person would show some pity;
> if only one would turn and comfort me.
> But instead, they give me poison for food;
> they offer me sour wine to satisfy my thirst.
> (Psalm 69:20-21 NLT)

The prophet Jeremiah in a moment of sheer frustration cries out to God and questions him.

> Why then does my suffering continue? Why is my wound so incurable? Your help seems as uncertain as a seasonal brook. It is like a spring that has gone dry. (Jeremiah 15:18 NLT)

It is hard to fathom the painful response of the heart when promises are broken or even delayed. Jeremiah feels like God's slow response is like a spring that has no water. His thirst, his anguish cannot be resolved or worse, it appears that God won't resolve it anytime soon. Hope is the necessary spring water of the soul which refreshes us and keeps us moving forward; without it, life is hard and meaningless. One can only walk in the desert of despair for so long. Living in between can be both frustrating and painful if our hearts have deferred hope for too long. At some point, the heart simply stops hoping and moves into a protective mode of simple survival. This mode of simple survival is better known as "soul murder," which is living a life where the heart no longer hopes, dreams, or longs for something more. The heart recoils and turns inward and life becomes a plastic shell of activities and responsibilities. After all, if one keeps his or her heart from longing or hoping, then the pain of disappointment will not be experienced.

"My Feet Were Slipping" (Psalm 73)

Questioning life is not new nor is it something the Bible glosses over with glib and plastic answers. The writers of Scripture struggled with life and even God at times. What is more amazing is Scripture records it in radical honesty. The Bible does not hide the weakness of its followers, their struggles with sin, God, and each other. This is one dynamic proof for the reliability of the Word of God. Normally people who are founding a new religion tend to gloss over the negatives of a particular work or persuasion by way of exclusion or rewriting (redacting) when they are trying to promote their religious beliefs or teachings. You know if you are going to market a new religion when you only want to show those elements that make your god and people look good and others look bad. Conversely, the Bible is not afraid to list the complaints of God's servants and their frustrations with His love and justice, or how He appears to not administer love and justice in an appropriate and timely manner.

This is one of the many reasons why we love the Bible. It does not hesitate at recording what actually happened, allowing for candid honesty, something the church of today could practice. As a matter of fact, it makes me grateful that the Scripture is no longer being written and collected today. It might read something like: "Pastor Mike Perkinson prayed and sought the Lord for many days as he contended for his people's welfare. However, in the second month he fell prey to depression and sank to the depths of despair, no longer being able to enter his pulpit and deliver the Word of God and encourage the people." "Pastor Tom Johnston prays for people for healing all the time and they are often healed, but he remains ill. What's with that?" Can we say the Bible does not flatter its characters with such depictions of honesty? Rather, it flatters the character and love of God in the lives of confused and broken sheep.

Nonetheless, life is hard to comprehend, especially when the world of promise seems to be operating like a delayed airline flight. You bought the ticket with the knowledge that the flight would leave at 2:37 p.m. on Thursday. It is now 4:45 p.m. with no sign of the plane. The airlines begin to give away roundtrip tickets for those who are inconvenienced and stranded and even a complimentary night at the local hotel. Such concessions are nice, but they in no way take away the frustration and problems a delayed flight causes. Hundreds of people attempt to alter their lives and schedules to the time frame provided by the airline. In the same way, there are many believers sitting at God's airport waiting for their plane to come. The arrival time is far beyond what they thought was promised or even reasonable for that matter. How long must we wait? "How long, O LORD, must I call for help? But you do not listen!" (Habakkuk 1:2 NLT). "When is my plane going to arrive?" "When is my promise going to come to pass?"

Exacerbating the problem is the issue of injustice. When will God make everything right? Balance the scales? Restore the balance in the force?

> ..."Violence!" I cry, but you do not come to save. Must I forever see this sin and misery all around me? Wherever I look, I see destruction and violence. I am surrounded by people who love to argue and fight. The law has become paralyzed and useless, and there is no justice given in the courts. The wicked far outnumber the righteous, and justice is perverted with bribes and trickery. (Habakkuk 1:2-4 NLT)

> You are perfectly just in this. But will you, who cannot allow sin in any form, stand idly by while they swallow us up? Should you be silent while the wicked destroy people who are more righteous than they? (Habakkuk 1:13 NLT)

> They called loudly to the Lord and said, "O Sovereign Lord, holy and true, how long will it be before you judge the people who belong to this world for what they have done to us? When will you avenge our blood against these people?" (Revelation 6:10 NLT)

The issue of justice being satisfied has been the heart's cry of countless millions in human history. Justice overlooked and wickedness promoted jades the soul while innocent hearts suffer at the hands of their tormentors. The Bible is not afraid to look in the direction of pain and suffering, even allowing the faithful servants of the Most High to question Him and His actions. God is not afraid or appalled at your questions or frustrated emotions. Maybe your cry for justice and righteousness is really nothing more than a reflection of the heart of God?

As we have seen, the prophets were not afraid to question God. Their faith in God was solid and submitted, allowing them to be themselves in relation to their Creator. True relationship cannot happen unless the self is genuine. Although they were questioning God, their hearts were never positioned to rebel or deny God. A great example of the relational dynamic is found in the complaint in the prophet Habakkuk, a complaint given so that God might answer. The prophet wants to hear from the Lord and is willing to respond to whatever God says.

> I trembled inside when I heard all this; my lips quivered with fear. My legs gave way beneath me, and I shook in terror. I will wait quietly for the coming day when disaster will strike the people who invade us. Even though the fig trees have no blossoms, and there are no grapes on the vine; even though the olive crop fails, and the fields lie empty and barren; even though the flocks die in the fields, and the cattle barns are empty, yet I will rejoice in the LORD! I will be joyful in the God of my salvation. (Habakkuk 3:16-18 NLT)

The heart of true faithfulness is demonstrated most clearly when life is not working out, when it appears that God is not involved in your life. It was Teresa of Avila, the sixteenth century saint, who said that real faith is that which believes when there is no reason to believe but belief itself. With this understood, maybe we can catch a glimpse at the beauty of a trial and the seasons of testing in our lives. They tend to purify our hearts and let us know just how strong our faith is and reveal quite clearly what or who our faith is in. It can be said that when the pressure is on what is contained within the heart will surface. Pressure or trials tend to squeeze out the real stuff of our souls.

Maybe what is needed more than ever in our day and age is an "impractical Christianity." That's right, a Christianity that doesn't work. Hold tight before you decide to throw the book down. We do understand that in our pragmatically driven culture the idea of a faith that doesn't work sounds useless and downright absurd. Why in the world would we follow a religious system that does not benefit our lives? Like everything else in life, we expect concrete, prompt, and measurable results from following Christ. Maybe it is true that God loves us and has a plan for our lives, but someone forgets to mention that His plan for us might be a difficult one, at least to understand.

Asaph, in Psalm 73, discovered the awesome presence and comfort of God in the midst of confusion and disillusionment. Asaph, in the midst of his struggle, asks the question many followers of Christ have asked -- has it been worth it? "Was it for nothing that I kept my heart pure and kept myself from doing wrong? All I get is trouble all day long; every morning brings me pain" (Psalm 73:13-14 NLT).

It is in this frustration and despair that Asaph discovers the answer to his dilemma will not necessarily come in this life, nor is the answer some great circumstantial gift. Rather, Asaph realizes in an eternal moment that the greatest gift he could have and that which makes life more clear is the presence of God himself. The vantage point or vista of God's presence is what brings clarity to this often confusing world.

> Then one day I went into your sanctuary, O God, and I thought about the destiny of the wicked.
> Truly, you put them on a slippery path
> and send them sliding over the cliff to destruction. In an instant they are destroyed,
> swept away by terrors.
> Their present life is only a dream
> that is gone when they awake.
> When you arise, O Lord,
> you will make them vanish from this life.
> (Ps. 73:17-20 NLT)

It would appear that God does some of his best work when we can't get life to work. It's as if the Lord would say to us:

> My child, you're in bondage to the Law of Linearity...the Principle of Sequence. It obligates you to do what's right to win the blessings you desire...that law has been replaced by the Law of Liberty. Under the Law of Liberty, you're free to live in the mystery of trust.
>
> But you haven't accepted the authority of this new law because it requires you to give up the illusion of control. You've cheapened the requirements of holiness by assuming you can do enough right things to bring about the Better Life. Sometimes that works. Sometimes it doesn't. You therefore live with uncertainty and pressure, and you demand to know the way to live that will make your life work as you want. You maneuver; you do not trust. You negoti-

> ate; you do not worship. You analyze and interpret to gain control over what happens; you do not depend. You see the Better Life of God's blessings over the Better Hope of God's presence. (Crabb, *The Pressure's Off* 7-8)

Asaph found that Law of Linearity broken once he found the Better Hope of God's presence. Somehow the mystery of discovering God's presence and having him fill our lives with hope and joy is the process by which we truly live and have a faith that really works. This is the key to living in between, the essential factor to living in the now of the Kingdom and in ultimately inheriting the Promise of the not yet.

CHAPTER THREE

The Need for Radical Trust: "Hurry Up and Die"

It is Not What is Lost, But What Is Gained

It has been said, "when a man knows God, losses and crosses cease to matter to him; what he has gained simply banishes these things from his mind" (Packer 23). It has been said that life is about attitude or perspective. It is what you see, or believe is real, that really matters. For the mature saint in Christ, trying to understand life is not the pursuit. Instead, the mature believer seeks to live in God's presence on a daily basis, allowing the hope that His presence removes the weight that life demands we carry.

There are two godly individuals we would like to introduce to you who were in many ways Mike's grandparents. Grandpa and Grandma Hansen served the Lord faithfully for many years. When Mike reflects upon their lives he sees Jesus. Like all of us, they experienced their share of pain and suffering, much of which was centered on their oldest grandson. The oldest grandson went through a season in his life where he was angry and rebellious. He seemed to do everything he could to bring pain and discord within the family. Grandma and Grandpa were always willing to be a place of refuge for their grandson, even when he was not reflecting the godly characteristics they desired. He would often be able to get money from his grandparents and would often take advantage of their mercy. In spite of this they did not feel like they had been ripped off by their grandson, even though he has borrowed a lot of money from them and realistically, used them. Their philosophy regarding the loss of money was extraordinary and simple. Life was about loving God and loving His people and in this case, it meant loving their grandson more than the money they had (which was not a lot). As Grandma said, "When you love someone, you are willing to do what is necessary."

How does one come into this state of right relationship with God where the heart is yielded no matter what happens? Obviously, the only entrance into a right relationship with God is through death (this will be expanded upon in a later chapter), the death and resurrection of Christ. As stated in John 14:6, He is the only Way. We are not simply citing a doctrinal statement here that the only way to salvation is Jesus Christ, but strongly asserting that the only way to live life is in proper relationship with the Way, Jesus. The Way is not merely a creedal declaration; He is a Person. We can do nothing except receive the atoning work. God gives us the grace to live in right relation with Him, His people, and His world and provides the Holy Spirit to engage life fully. This is what Jesus was pointing to when He was speaking in Acts 1:8. As Paul writes, "that God, by his power, will fulfill all your good intentions and faithful deeds" (2 Thessalonians 1:11b NLT). As you can see, it is by God's power and our faith or trust in Him that is the formula for righteous living. He does it. He is the source of all power and life (Acts 17:28; Colossians 1:15-17). Our role in the relationship is to trust Him, believe what He says, and live our lives based on it. Let us clarify this here; we are not suggesting five steps to maximizing your life (the Law of Linearity) or how to get what you want from God based on living a blessed life. We are not talking about adding God to the matrix of your life. Rather, we are strongly stating that to live life in this manner is to love God with your whole heart, which would result in basing your entire life around God and His Kingdom - seeking first the King and His Kingdom (Matthew 6:33).

Since we are dealing with a person in God, as is the case with all relationships, proper response is required. In our case, "we love because he first loved us" (1 John 4:19). Our response to that love is then to receive it and give it back with our lives. We could break down our response by seeking God's presence on a daily, moment by moment basis. We can best do this by:

Loving God with all of the self (Matthew 22:37-38). Make Him the primary focus of our life. Scripture makes it clear that God is the source of our lives, and life cannot be fully lived and enjoyed unless we are in right relationship with Him.

Loving others as yourself (Matthew 22:39-40). If we are in right relationship with God, then we will be in right relationship with the self, which will allow us to truly love others.

As you live, make disciples (Matthew 28:18-20). We make disciples best when we live as daily followers of Jesus. Doing so ignites hope in our souls and allows our lives to shout hope so loudly that others will hear and might even inquire (1 Peter 3:15; Matthew 5:13-16). Is anyone asking about the hope that lies within you? We know, such a rude question, after all, how can you have hope when your own hope has been delayed?

Seek to trust God with your life and not control Him or your life. You cannot control anything, as we said - *all control is an illusion* - so why try? The best way to trust Him is by living in the moment. Don't try to control the outcome of life - *freefall into your future* - trusting Him to catch you. We can only live in the moment like this when our past is resolved or released and our future is hopeful. Jesus offers some wise advice here as He says, "So don't worry about tomorrow, for tomorrow will bring its own worries. Today's trouble is enough for today" (Matthew 6:34 NLT).

How do you live in the moment like this? Through His abiding presence. Make your heart a chapel where you can go at anytime to talk with God. The more we live in the moment the more we are free from our past and hopeful about our future. The more we accept and settle our past the more hope we have for our future, which allows us to live in the present moment.

Realize you are dependent and needy and confess it on a daily basis (Matthew 6:9-13). *This closes the door to the past and opens the door to the future.* It goes against the grain of our human nature but is the key to living life in between. Jesus made it quite clear in the Lord's Prayer that one of our daily requests needs to be for our sustenance, "give us our food for today" (Matthew 6:11 NLT). Logically, at least for us, it would be better to ask God for a storehouse so that we might store our food supplies in large quantities. That way we would not need to trouble Him on such mundane matters and could then occupy our prayer time with more significant matters. After all, maximizing our time and being ever so efficient with our lives is of utmost importance and critical for our lives to be productive. Apparently this does not matter as much to God as it does to us. One tends to think that Jesus told us to pray daily for our food and basic needs, not because God cannot or will not do a storehouse, but that we need to come to Him on a daily basis. The source of our lives is not in the self or a storehouse, but in God. This does not imply that saving or planning is wrong, it means Jesus builds into our daily prayer a vaccine against self-trust. Thank God for storehouses. Just remember who provides the stuff you have stacked up in it!

We will talk more later on how to overcome life and the in between's. For now, let it suffice to say that we need to learn what it means to have a proper response to God.

What Happened?

One of the great tragedies of life is the lack of victory and joy many feel as believers. Maybe this is due to the human need to live between the polarities of active voice (controlling life) or the passive voice (giving up on life and letting it happen to you). We shall look at this in more detail in a few chapters. Suffice it to say for now that we call this lack of joy and victory a tragedy because of the provision God has granted us in Christ. We have been given the keys to life and still are unable to unlock the door and step through to a life of freedom. "The glory of God is a human being fully alive" wrote Irenaeus in the Second Century (quoted in Eldredge 10). If any should reveal what it truly means to be a human being on this planet, it is the followers of Jesus. The Son of God did not come to establish a new religion but to restore the sons and daughters back to the Father. This restoration of the Kingdom takes place in our hearts and those who have been restored to the King shine the brightest in the dark world, shedding the light of hope for all to embrace. After all, we are to be light and salt (Matthew 5:13-16) to this world and living so loudly that people would ask us of the hope that is within us (1 Peter 3:15). We asked before -- do you recall the last time someone asked you about the hope that is within you? Do we live loud enough? What has happened to cause many sons and daughters of the King to fall prey to such a drab, dreary, routine, and pressure-based life that often lacks joy and peace? If Jesus came to bring hope and joy, then why aren't there more parties and simple celebrations of life?

As we have noted, there is something within human nature that struggles to continue, especially when one feels they have been swimming upstream for a long period of time - life in between is most difficult at this juncture. At some point we all get tired, disillusioned and discouraged, leading to the tragedy of giving up. Satan would love to wear you down and destroy any life of Jesus that exists in you, to nullify the seed's growth before it can really settle in. Swimming upstream may be a problem, but is it possible that God may not want us in the stream?

Maybe the greatest problem of all is that we are afraid to plunge into the unknown and the painful, what life often is, and so we live in the active or passive voice, choosing denial as the medication to ease the disappointment of the delayed promise. We do this instead of facing life and attempting to live in the middle voice, not controlling life or giving up on it, but simply engaging and participating with life and God. However, when the demise of the promise seems certain and all that is left is the sheer truth of God's love and presence coupled with the faint hope of heaven, rather than joy filling our hearts, what tends to happen for many is a cosmic sadness overtakes the soul. The larger questions of life loom over us, demanding answers that we cannot give. And yet we are hesitant to wrestle with them. Max Lucado writes:

> How in the world can a person be born, be educated, fall in or out of love, have a job, be married, give birth, raise kids, see death, retire, and die without ever, ever asking why? Never asking, 'Why am I here?' Or, worse yet, asking why and being content with no answer.
>
> History is jam-packed with lives that died with no purpose. Neighborhoods reek with mediocrity. Office complexes are painted gray with boredom. Nine-to-fivers are hypnotized by routine.
>
> But does anyone object? Does anyone defy the machinery? Does anyone ask why? Sometimes I want to stand at the corner of the street and yell, 'Doesn't anyone want to know why? Why lonely evenings? Why broken hearts? Why abandoned marriages? Why fatherless babies?'
>
> But I never yell it. I just stick my hands in my pockets and stare . . . and wonder.
>
> The most deadly trick of Satan is not to rob us of answers. It's to steal our questions. (*On the Anvil* 32-33)

God has more for us than many of us realize. His plans are much larger than we care to think. Pastor and President of the International Church of the Foursquare Gospel churches in Sri Lanka, Leslie Keegle, had a vision during a pastor's conference for one of the Foursquare churches in the United States. In the vision, Keegle said there was an eagle that was chained with its wings clipped and a snake that was laughing at the eagle saying, "I won't hurt you if you let me stay" (Overman).

The message to this church involved their destiny which was to be an eagle that soared. Unfortunately, they had settled for something less than what God had for them. The church had grown to a point that the world would have called successful, doing many things well and even impacting the community. In so doing, the congregation grew to live more in their accomplishments than in their call. We often wonder just how many believers are living a life that is far less than what God has called them to embrace, no longer soaring as eagles but living below the plane of experience and life that we were originally created for.

Clarification for Your Journey

In this whole journey through life, through the "Land of In Between," what God wants from us is our hearts, our passions, and our longings. Maybe it would be better to say, our dreams, hopes, and aspirations. These are relational realities that require a different posture of heart than what compliance, mental assent, or behavioral change demands. If God is a person (and He is, and desires our hearts) it is rather apparent that what is necessary is that we must become sons and daughters in relationship with their Father in Heaven. That is, we must be

> worshipers before workers; indeed the only acceptable workers are those who have learned the lost art of worship. It is inconceivable that a sovereign and holy God should be so hard up for workers that He would press into service anyone who had been empowered regardless of his moral qualifications. (Tozer 37)

There is a lot of instruction and teaching in our day and age on how to live better for our Lord but very little that is healthy and biblical on how to die to the self. We realize there is a morbid stream of teaching that bathes its listeners in the painful waters of condemnation as it utilizes guilt to motivate its followers to die to the self. We are not implying in any way that we spend our time with a defeatist gospel that lends itself to destroying the faith and identity of the individual with a constant barrage of negativity, making it clear we are worthless sinners.

The Bible makes it clear that we do not deserve God's love and mercy but that is a far cry from whether or not we have worth. The simple fact that Jesus gave His life indicates the value we have to God. We are not worthy in the sense of earning His love, but we are of great worth simply because He loves us and deems us worthy. For example, the work of Van Gogh or Michelangelo has great worth; it is the work of the artist that makes it worthwhile, not the state it is in. We say this to clarify that when we are referring to "dying to the self" we are not arguing for "worm" theology, which speaks about our absolute wickedness. We agree and understand that we have fallen from the place God originally intended, but we are still created by the Divine Artist and worth something because we have been created by Him and fashioned in His image. The signature of God is on every human life, more accurately called the "Image of God" given to all, as the ancient book of Genesis declares.

It becomes clear then that God's current agenda is about restoration, and as the King He desires to restore His Kingdom and will do so one day in fullness. Sons and daughters of a King are princes and princesses. We are all fallen princes and princesses in need of restoration to our original design and purpose. God desires to restore us to that place, but it cannot happen unless we die to the self and live the life He created us for. We believe the church needs to hear in fresh ways what it means to lay its flesh down and die daily. By "flesh" we are referring to those human plans of the heart to maintain itself outside of God (control), not our physical existence per se. As has become most apparent, it is during the in between of life that we find our heart struggling most for control. After all, God is not coming through and, like any discouraged or disillusioned soul, we pick up the pieces, pull up our boot straps and take care of our lives. Like oxygen deprived individuals, we clamor and strain for that last breath, fighting to create alternate means of air supply, backup systems and the like, instead of trusting the air that God has so graciously promised. What we really need to do is just hurry up and die, letting go of the control, and trusting God to raise us up to newness in life. This kind of release, of giving ourselves to God, is essential to inherit what He has for us. It is only then that God will cause the fresh breath of His life to flow into us and our life, sustaining us while we live in between.

In many ways, it is as ridiculous as a fish deciding to live outside the environment it was created to exist in, the water. Allow us a moment of foolishness. Mr. Fish has intelligence and decides to build air filters and water supplies that allow it to exist on land. It strains for its survival rather than swimming in the vast waters already created for it by God. We in the same manner, seek to find our own source of life as the prophet Jeremiah so aptly describes:

> For my people have done two evil things: They have forsaken me- the fountain of living water. And they have dug for themselves cracked cisterns that can hold no water at all!" (2:13 NLT)

The life of control, in which the life of in between almost demands we partake, is exactly what Jeremiah is addressing. People or fish, if you will, would rather walk on land than swim in the vast waters where life is provided, stress is non-existent or at least minimal, and all we need for life is before us. God has given us a well that will never run dry, but we strangely opt for broken wells that leak and need constant, daily attention. No wonder people in the church and the world are so stressed out. Maintaining one's well is hard work and rather ridiculous since a well with a better and constant water supply for life is already provided. It is precisely this attitude of control that needs to be surrendered and allowed to die, especially in the season of in between we all experience. After all it was Jesus who said, "...unless a grain of wheat falls into the ground and dies, it remains alone; but if it dies, it produces much grain" (John 12:24 NKJV). Maybe it is this need to control our own lives that God is trying to quietly remove so that we might learn to enjoy the fullness of life in Christ that is promised.

It is important for us to clarify here that the way one comes to know God is by faith. The writer of Hebrews makes it clear that faith is absolutely necessary when coming to God: "And without faith it is impossible to please him," (Hebrews 11:6a). By faith we do not mean simply creedal affirmations, although they are essential to faith, for one must believe in the right God, thus possessing, in one sense, a creedal affirmation or idea of some sort before faith can be exercised. What makes faith so dynamic is not the right creedal affirmation as it is the person and truth that affirmation points to. Right information is important and even vital but a person, at least initially, can be known without someone's knowing everything about them. When we speak of faith, we are not referring to the ability to convince oneself that black is white or that something will come to pass if we believe hard enough. Rather, faith is aligning our minds and hearts with Him; to what is true; to His way; to the person of Jesus. It is placing oneself into the very character of God and allowing that character to direct one's life. Faith can best be described as trust.

As we have noted, trusting what we have received is not as easy as it sounds. Too frequently, the language of trust has been reduced to nothing more than verbal declarations and window dressing of the act of faith. Simply, trust is rare these days. Modern faith is often without trust. For modern man, it is one thing to believe something entirely -- another to trust it. Biblically, this separation is not a part of the language of faith. Trust and faith represent opposite sides of the same coin - one total reality with two distinct facets.

We are in desperate need of re-discovering what it means to "trust" in God again; a second conversion is needed. Conversion involves two aspects, a turning toward something or someone and a turning away from something or someone. When conversion deals with turning toward God, we are learning to turn away from the trust of the world, the flesh (ourselves) and the Devil. We are to turn away from ourselves as the primary sustainers of life as we slowly but surely realize that God is truly the foundation and source of our lives and of everything that exists in this universe.

What is needed is what Brennan Manning calls "ruthless trust." It is ruthless because it is a trust that does not have the lasting fragrance, or odor of self-pity that so plagues our modern culture. It refuses to regard self-interest as the highest good in life, and recognizes that it has come to the end of itself and found its beginning in Jesus Christ. In this faith is the exact opposite of a heart that seeks to depend on itself.

And yet complicating this matter of trust is the in between of life which all too often involves not only waiting but pain and suffering. "How can I trust in God when our world is not safe, people are not trustworthy, and God seems to operate on a plane I don't understand?" It is these realities that often become the trust-breaking anguish of many struggling seekers.

The prophet Haggai helps us understand why life might not be working out for many as he graphically paints a picture of people who have moved away from trusting God to trusting and building their own lives. We were designed for something else and live far below that.

> Now this is what the LORD Almighty says: "Give careful thought to your ways. You have planted much, but have harvested little. You eat, but never have enough. You drink, but never have your fill. You put on clothes, but are not warm. You earn wages, only to put them in a purse with holes in it."
>
> This is what the LORD Almighty says: "Give careful thought to your ways. Go up to the mountains and bring down timber and build the house, so that I may take pleasure in it and be honored," says the LORD. "You expected much, but see, it turned out to be little. What you brought home, I blew away. Why?" declares the LORD Almighty. "Because of my house, which remains a ruin, while each of you is busy with his own house. Therefore, because of you the heavens have withheld their dew and the earth its crops. (Haggai 1:5-10 NIV)

The prophet makes us painfully aware that our lives can easily be spent in attempting to fill the void within, especially when we find ourselves living in between promise and fulfillment.

C. S. Lewis in book four of his classic, *The Chronicles of Narnia*, tells of a little girl named Jill who is lost in a rather scary forest and in need of a drink. She stumbles upon a stream and quickly runs toward it only to find a Lion lying beside it. The Lion knows she is thirsty and invites her to take a drink. For Jill to do this she must overcome her fear that the Lion might actually devour her.

> "May I-could I-would you mind going away while I do?" said Jill. The Lion answered this only by a look and a very low growl. And as Jill gazed at its motionless bulk, she realized that she might as well have asked the whole mountain to move aside for her convenience. The delicious rippling noise of the stream was driving her nearly frantic.
> "Will you promise not to-do anything to me, if I do come?" said Jill.
> "I make no promise," said the Lion.
> Jill was so thirsty now that, without noticing it, she had come a step nearer.
> "Do you eat girls?" she said.
> "I have swallowed up girls and boys, women and men, kings and emperors, cities and realms," said the Lion. It didn't say this as if it were boasting, nor as if it were sorry, nor as if were angry. It just said it.
> "I daren't come and drink," said Jill.
> "Then you will die of thirst," said the Lion.
> "Oh dear!" said Jill, coming another step nearer. "I suppose I must go and look for another stream then."
> "There is no other stream," said the Lion.
> (Lewis, *The Silver Chair* 17)

Jill, like many of us, asks for the promise of security, a promise that the Lion is not willing to give. She needs the promise to satisfy her thirst. She is willing to forego the stream, the only stream, to give in to her need of a promise from the Lion that she will be safe. The Lion, like Christ, promises fullness, that our inner thirst will be satisfied, with hope, life, etc., a promise that many, like Jill, will bypass because our condition has not been met. Unfortunately, there are no other streams in life, only temporary thirst relievers that distract us from the harsh reality that our souls are dry and long for the water that will satisfy our insatiable thirst.

In order for Jill to drink she must not only believe the Lion is real, that he exists, but trust him. She must place her life, her safety, her future in the hands of this large and ferocious beast who only provides an invitation to drink, to bring satisfaction to her thirsty soul. Like Jill, we must trust God with our lives, our safety, and our future, which feels almost impossible to do when you feel trapped in the in between.

The irony is that it is in this place of in between; we discover trust in its purest form. We realize during this time what or who we really trust and what our lives are truly about, which may be why it is so painful for us. The degree of pain we experience is not only due to a personal loss or the length of time it is taking God to act, but to the sobering thought that we are not in control of our lives as we once thought. Being responsible for our lives is one thing, but control is another and during our short or long seasons of living in between our control centers are short circuited and destroyed. We either take a drink from the water (the fountain of living water) guarded by the Lion or search in vain for another stream (broken cisterns).

The way trust is best encountered is through encountering the gracious love of God. Through this love a person experiences the irreversible forgiveness of Jesus through an act of trust which allows that person to be redeemed from the corrosive power of fear. Moving from mistrust to trust is a daily process whereby we step away from the warehouse of worry and trust our very lives to the One who has wonderfully saved and forgiven us. This is easier said than done, particularly for those who have encountered a serious violation of trust by other human beings, which may explain why faith is so hard for some. The same mechanism that releases the heart to trust a person is the one we utilize to trust God. If our hearts have been injured or our trust mechanisms violated in some way, then to trust again is a frightening process that reminds the soul that the last time we did this we were crushed, forgotten, abandoned, unloved, and hurt. Living in the in between of life can easily be interpreted by such a person that God has forgotten or abandoned them; that He does not really love them or has decided against them. We will talk more about this later.

Let us list for you some basic signs of mistrust or, as many would say, lack of faith.

Issues with the self: Always worried about what others think; overly concerned with appearance, acceptance, and being appreciated. This self concern can take two forms: a low view of the self, self-hate, self-rejection or an inflated self-centered, narcissistic view of the self.

Unhealthy shame, guilt, self-condemnation, and remorse: A way we overcompensate for our pain and disillusionment is to lay blame on the self. This is another form of control. It would be like getting into a fight with someone who could hurt you. Since you are not afraid of the damage they may cause, the unknown factor, you inflict pain on yourself, the known factor. To ensure that the pain level stays within controllable parameters you then knock yourself out. Here are the controllable parameters - first, we consider ourselves all bad, blaming the self for everything that has gone wrong in our lives. "God is not providing because I am bad." Or we consider ourselves all good and blame family, society, God, etc., for the situation(s) we are in.

Controlling: Inability or unwillingness to believe or trust anyone would really follow through and do what they said they would do. We can live lives of control in two ways: First, we can take charge of everything and be manipulative, controlling - the active voice; or we can be the "life happens to me" person, skeptical and cynical - the passive voice (the victim). Finally, we can choose to become the "I don't care" or "whatever" (detached or apathetic) person, giving up our longings and wishes and living with no opinion or desire. The logic to this life posture is simple: a heart can only hurt or be disappointed if it longs for something. And so, the key to a life without pain is to kill one's longings, soul murder.

Angry and unforgiving: When we live in between the core of our soul is often exposed and so is what drives it. As a result, we can become angry because we are not getting what we want. The anger can be justified to some degree but also can be nothing more than sophisticated pouting. What is revealed is what is driving the heart: Anger results when we find the focus of our pursuit blocked. Or we employ "protective emotion." Anger then compensates to help pump us up, make us bigger to handle the challenge. This can be good if danger is present but can be harmful if we become the danger. That is, a danger to ourselves, not referring to suicidal thoughts necessarily, but to giving in to the driving forces of the self which are in opposition to God and His desires for us. Finally, we come to the place where unforgiveness destroys the heart by allowing us to protect our hearts from further pain only to destroy it as it does so.

The basis of biblical trust is the conviction that God is good, wants us to grow, to unfold, and to experience fullness in life. Simply, He wants to bless us and has already done so through Jesus, the yes of God. God by definition is thinking of me. Something about God's existence involves His thoughts of us. Jesus made that clear when He said:

> What is the price of five sparrows? A couple of pennies? Yet God does not forget a single one of them. And the very hairs on your head are all numbered. So don't be afraid; you are more valuable to him than a whole flock of sparrows. (Luke 12:6-7 NLT)

This kind of trust does not happen overnight and unfortunately is acquired through a series of crises and trials. Hold tight and brace yourself: *trust is purified in the crucible of trial.* King David, the beloved king of Jewish history, was no stranger to living in the in between as he experienced terror, loneliness, failure, familial discord, and even malicious attempts to undermine and destroy him. And yet he somehow found peace and refreshment in the heart of God with his unwavering trust.

> But when I am afraid,
> I put my trust in you.
> O God, I praise your word.
> I trust in God, so why should I be afraid?
> What can mere mortals do to me? (Psalm 56:3-4 NLT)

> He led me to a place of safety;
> he rescued me because he delights in me. (Psalm 18:19 NLT)

> But I trust in your unfailing love.
> I will rejoice because you have rescued me. (Psalm 13:5 NLT)

> Wait patiently for the LORD.
> Be brave and courageous.
> Yes, wait patiently for the LORD. (Psalm 27:14 NLT)

> But I am like an olive tree,
> thriving in the house of God.
> I trust in God's unfailing love
> forever and ever.
> I will praise you forever, O God,
> for what you have done.
> I will wait for your mercies
> in the presence of your people. (Psalm 52:8-9 NLT)

The apostle John, known as the beloved disciple, helps us understand how to come to such a life of trust as he writes: "We know how much God loves us, and we have put our trust in him" (1 John 4:16a NLT). The key to trusting God is in knowing how much He loves you. John makes it quite clear that "we love because he first loved us" (1 John 4:19). This is a knowledge that does not come by memorized repetition of verses or a rigid discipline only, but by experiencing the person of Jesus Christ through the power of the Holy Spirit.

Biblical transformation always comes by way of encounter with God. Job encapsulates this for us with his humble response to God after the barrage of questions that made it clear to Job that the God he was dealing with was far greater than he had originally thought. All this allowed him to be transformed because of his personal encounter with God which allowed him to repent, adjust his life and worldview, and live accordingly.

> I had heard about you before, but now I have seen you with my own eyes. I take back everything I said, and I sit in dust and ashes to show my repentance. (Job 42:5-6)

It is precisely this uncompromising trust in the love of God that inspires us to live with gratitude and hope during our season of in between. Even when spiritual darkness envelopes us, this uncompromising trust allows us to pray from the heart, "Abba Father ("dad" for us today), I entrust my past, present and future into your hands, choosing to live in the moment. Whatever you want of me, I want of me. Into your care I entrust my frail, distracted, insecure, and tentative heart. Abba Father, unto you I abandon myself in Jesus our Lord. Amen."

The way of trust is best described as a process. One does not come by the way of trust through meticulous scrutiny, religious zeal or fanatical bibliolatry. Rather, one comes the way of trust through the avenue of obscurity. It is through this undefined and ambiguous path that we find the way of trust, not the clearly marked path for the future that we all crave and seek to find. What drives these pilgrims to continue to trust God in the in between of life, to venture out into uncertainty leaving what is permanent, secure, and obvious for what seems so irrational and unsure, is the simple heartfelt response that God has not only initiated the movement but has offered his presence as the seal of His promise (Ephesians 1:13-14).

The sad fact however, is most Christians, as we have already demonstrated, are no different in their attitudes and emotions than those who do not have relationship with Christ. For those whose thirst is to be satisfied by the "living water" it is amazing how thirsty those in Christ remain. Either the water is bad (think not) or we have not learned to really drink from the "fountain of living water" on a regular and frequent basis.

In some ways, we are in a situation that is really no different than Jonathan Edwards encountered in 1727 when he took over his grandfather Stoddard's congregation. He tells us they were "dry bones," possessing a form of godliness but denying its power. As Edwards saw them, they were respectable people who possessed a kind of rote orthodoxy, shuffling doctrines like a deck of cards. The problem was their ultimate goals and desires did not involve the Kingdom of God, but affluence and the acquiescence of land. We need to clarify here that we do not believe that affluence or even owning land is evil nor did Edwards. Rather, the issue is what drives us or as Jesus said, "Wherever your treasure is, there your heart and thoughts will also be" (Matthew 6:21 NLT). Their children were given to night walking and tavern hunting; no doubt, if drugs had existed, they would have used them (taken from Lovelace 37-42).

Many in our circle might be caught up in the race of acquiring money, things, etc., as well as lured into the ideology of the day that tells us that personal happiness and comfort is the chief end of humanity. There is a quiet sense that tells us we deserve to be happy and therefore it is our right. What is a right easily becomes a demand which then creates pressure, stress, relational tension. Need we go on? Marriages, in turn, have become a contractual compromise instead of relationships built on love and sacrifice. After all, if we are first and foremost in pursuit of happiness and comfort, then all of life should somehow facilitate this. Something in the in between of life makes this rather difficult.

Dr. Larry Crabb peels back the layers of denial by poignantly speaking the truth. Before we quote Dr. Crabb we feel that we need to provide a warning label for you. Danger: The following comment will be hazardous to denial, pride, and self-centered mentalities. Can cause death to the flesh, or just make you mad. Well, if you do get mad, remember Dr. Crabb said it, not us!

> In all of it, the point of things seems to be us, not God. How we're getting along at any moment seems more important than whether we're connecting with God. And when we do think about connecting with God, we tend to be more concerned with what's in it for us than with finding real power and clearer vision so we can better further His purposes. (Crabb, *Cry of the Soul*, Foreword 9)

Since spiritual transformation begins with an encounter with God, an encounter that results in an honest disclosure of the self which is the process that leads to repentance, we then see that confession (the denial destroyer) is the beginning process for spiritual growth, healing, and transformation. More simply, we begin by being honest and that is precisely what a life in between does. It forces us to ponder honestly the reality of our lives, our relationship with God, and what the ruling passion of our heart is.

Let's return to Jonathan Edwards, as he goes on to describe, in his work, Faithful Narrative of the Surprising Work of God, how God began to change the hearts of the young people, who then went home and told their parents. From this, the dead orthodoxy of the people in the church began to come alive. The gravity of the covetousness that once possessed them, this drive to be affluent and to acquire, was no longer the main focus of their lives. Instead, they became consumed with the things of God to the point that the business men of the day even began to neglect their businesses to talk about God. Songs of praise fell from their lips as they now sang hymns out of delight instead of duty. Overtaken by the powerful and gracious love of God, the once duty-bound congregants found renewed zeal that released their hearts to share this new found freedom with others (taken from Lovelace 38-39).

> The illumination of the heart which brought converts in touch with the reality of God simultaneously revealed to them how deeply sin gripped their own lives. They suddenly became aware that their problem was not isolated acts of conscious disobedience to God, but a deep aversion to God at the root of their personalities, selfishness, jealousy and other underlying complexes of sin. Some were in agony-even convicted because they were not more sensibly convicted-until they broke through to the realization that the only righteousness that could reconcile such depravity to a holy God was that of Jesus Christ, who offered himself for them on the cross. (Lovelace 38-39)

Dietrich Bonhoeffer takes the thought even further as he writes about how we have cheapened grace. Keep in mind that Bonhoeffer made this assertion in the 1930's. We'll take a moment to let him say it. This might be a little painful to hear. Hold tight and prayerfully listen.

> Cheap Grace is the deadly enemy of our Church. We are fighting today for costly grace.

> Cheap Grace means grace sold on the market like cheapjack's wares. The sacraments, the forgiveness of sin, and the consolation of religion are thrown away at cut prices. Grace is presented as the Church's inexhaustible treasury, from which she showers blessings with generous hands, without asking questions or fixing limits.

Grace without price; grace without cost! The essence of grace, we suppose, is that the account has been paid in advance; and, because it has been paid, everything can be had for nothing. Since the cost was infinite, the possibilities of using and spending it are infinite. What would grace be if it were not cheap?

...In such a Church the world finds a cheap covering for its sins; no contrition is required, still less any real desire to be delivered from sin. Cheap grace therefore amounts to a denial of the living Word of God, in fact, a denial of the Incarnation of the Word.

Cheap grace means justification of sin without justification of the sinner...Cheap grace is the preaching of forgiveness without requiring repentance, baptism without church discipline, Communion without confession, absolution without personal confession. Cheap grace is grace without discipleship, grace without the cross, grace without Jesus Christ, living and incarnate.

Costly grace is the treasure hidden in the field; for the sake of it a man will gladly go and sell all that he has. It is the pearl of great price to buy which the merchant will sell all his goods. It is the kingly rule of Christ, for whose sake a man will pluck out the eye which causes him to stumble, it is the call of Jesus Christ at which the disciple leaves his nets and follows him.

Costly grace is the gospel which must be sought again and again, the gift which must be asked for, the door at which a man must knock.

Such grace is costly because it calls us to follow, and it is grace because it calls us to follow Jesus Christ. It is costly because it costs a man his life, and it is grace because it gives a man the only true life. It is costly because it condemns sin and grace because it justifies the sinner. Above all, it is costly because it cost God the life of his Son: 'ye were bought at a price,' and what has cost God much cannot be cheap for us. Above all, it is grace because God did not reckon his Son too dear a price to pay for our life, but delivered him up for us. Costly grace is the Incarnation of God. (Bonhoeffer, *The Cost of Discipleship* 45-48)

Our culture is in danger of making grace cheap. Some would argue that we have already made it cheap, marketing a Jesus who will meet all your needs, bless your life, your plans, and secure your health and wealth if you simply acknowledge Him as savior. Or as the liberal Al Franken has called it, the "Supply-Side Jesus", a Jesus that is republican, white, middle-class, and conservative; this is a political and economically beneficial Jesus (Franken 313) but not necessarily the same Jesus of the Gospels. Donald Miller writes honestly when he says,

> ...it makes me wonder if secretly we don't wish God were a genie who could deliver a few wishes here and there. And that makes me wonder if what we really want from the formulas are the wishes, not God. It makes me wonder if what we really want is control, not a relationship...Some would say formulas are how we interact with God, that going through motions and jumping through hoops are how a person acts out his spirituality. (12-13)

We are going so far as to say that in many ways our Christian culture has already cheapened grace by making Christianity more about the formulas, the behavior and the blessings, instead of a relationship with God. After all, is that not the main thrust of our frustration in the in between, questioning God because we have performed our end of the bargain, followed His principles, been obedient, faithful, which can only mean that it is now His turn to provide the blessing He promised. Having said that, let us take a moment and provide three simple categories that might help us understand where we might be on the "cheap grace" scale. The Christianity of our day can be categorized as follows:

Carnal Christian: A person who may know Christ, go to church, know their Bible and even read it, and lives a fairly self-centered life, doing what they feel is right for the moment. This person honors God in name and title, but not in devotion. Jesus is not the center of their lives. They don't behave like a Christian outside of church, but only do so during religious services. Their hearts are calloused and controlling and their thought life is far from that of Jesus.

Cultural Christian: A person who is moral and behaves as Christ would on issues of morality adopts the cultural values they live in without really knowing what they are, and even seeks to find scripture to support and validate it. This person may be kind but not necessarily loving, may be gracious but not necessarily giving. The Cultural Christian is focused more on the benefits of being a Christian and therefore, seeks to understand all the principles and formulas of the faith so that blessing will result. Their relationship with God is much more like a business arrangement, where both parties agree to terms and commit to those terms, or like a drug fix wherein the person seeks to have Jesus provide a comfort fix through worship, something mood altering that makes them feel better. Worship and serving God becomes about the high and not necessarily God. Jesus is not the center of this person's life. They may behave like a Christian but they still do not have the heart and mind of a Christian - they don't think like Christ yet.

Christ-centered Christian: A person devoted to Jesus and whose life decisions are based on the Kingdom of God. A Christ-centered Christian is not perfect, but is seeking to be more like Jesus in their heart, attitude, and most of all, in how they love others. Jesus is the center of this person's life. They may not always behave like Christ, and when such occurs, they find their hearts broken and are quick to repent and come before God and others to confess this and allow God's transforming love to forgive and change them.

As you can see, the Carnal and Cultural Christians are not Kingdom driven or motivated by love, but driven more by desire, duty, and dollars. Let us clarify here that we are not saying it is wrong to enjoy culture or the pleasures God has created for us, or for that matter, there is nothing immoral with attempting to be complete and healthy. The problem is when it becomes the primary goal of the Christian; instead of pleasing the Father it indicates a deficient faith. In this sense, the life of balance and health must be submitted to the greater element of obedience to Jesus.

Before we go on we need to meddle a bit and make a bold pronouncement: *balance is a lie.* There is no such thing as balance when it comes to our lives. Life can be described as healthy but it is hard to describe a life as balanced. To balance life means that one must be in control of it, and as we said earlier, all control is an illusion. Balance requires our effort: We try to have some of this, but not too much of that, *and in doing so we miss the fullness of life God has for us.* Such fullness is our goal. As we understand the Bible, it seems to be telling us that we are to be radically dependent on God for our very lives. It is not balance that we are to seek after but His fullness - holiness, spiritual health, loving Him, loving others and passing on that love and life to others as we live our lives. We embrace this fullness, all the while trusting Him in the in between for the not yet of the Kingdom to come in its fullness.

CHAPTER FOUR

The Issue of Timing: "The Three Mile An Hour God"*

*"Three Mile An Hour God" is a book written by Kosuke Koyama

Trusting God When Our Questions Are Still Unanswered

As long as we question God's character without the ability to bring our questions into submission, our faith will remain tentative and uncertain. True faith or as we have been saying, trust enters the scene when evidence suggests that God is not about working His good will, when evidence implies that God will fail or that He does not care anymore or never did. More specifically trust finds its purest expression in seasons in between. To help the believer find the joy and life he/she was designed for, to die to the self, and trust God during the in between of life, is this tool of faith. Faith is a posture of the heart which is able to place itself into the care of God when everything tells it not to. Faith believes the Father and drinks from the cup He gives, because faith believes in His character and therefore, trusting Him with its very life. Faith is a personal matter and involves our trust of the person of God as Paul so clearly articulates: "...But I am not ashamed of it, for I know the one in whom I trust, and I am sure that he is able to guard what I have entrusted to him until the day of his return" (2 Timothy 1:12 NLT).

It is safe to say, the more evidence one needs, the less faith it requires to believe. When it comes to faith an element of risk is always involved. Ultimately, we must risk and lose our lives so that they may be found. The antithesis to faith or trust (as we have noted) is living a life of control that is most often expressed in our quest for clarity, the need to not only see where our next steps in life will take us but to select the path and speed of our journey.

John Kavanaugh, the brilliant ethicist went to work for three months at "the house of the dying" in Calcutta. He went to Calcutta seeking a clear answer as to how to best spend the rest of his life. He was hopeful that Mother Teresa could shed some light on his future. On the first morning there he met Mother Teresa. She asked, "And what can I do for you?" Kavanaugh asked her to pray for him. "What do you want me to pray for?" she asked. He then proceeded to voice the request that he had carried with him from the United States. He made his prayer request known at that moment, "Pray that I have clarity." Mother Teresa responded firmly, "No, I will not do that." When he asked her why, she said, "Clarity is the last thing you are clinging to and must let go." Kavanaugh proceeded to then make the comment that she always seemed to have the clarity he longed for. At which point, she laughed and said, "I have never had clarity, what I have always had is trust. So I will pray that you trust God" (quoted in Manning 5).

Like Kavanaugh, when we crave clarity what we are really doing is attempting to eliminate the risk of trusting God, which is another way of controlling our lives. Fear of the unknown path stretching ahead of us destroys the childlike trust in the Father's active goodness and unrestricted love. Compounding the difficulty of trust is the belief that many hold that having trust will dispel confusion, illuminate the darkness, vanquish the uncertainty, and redeem our lives, making the in between of life shorter and more bearable. Those three secret steps to spirituality that will usher in final and total fulfillment, allowing you to experience heaven on earth. In other words, everything will be ok when I trust, meaning that whatever bad is happening will no longer be happening when I trust God. The in between of life will end and I will experience the fullness of the promise I have been awaiting.

Unfortunately, the crowd of witnesses in Hebrews 11 strongly challenges this notion. Trust does not bring final clarity on this earth, as we all live in the not yet of the Kingdom of God. It does not calm the chaos or even dull the pain of life, or provide a crutch that allows us to limp along in it. Trusting God brings fullness, peace, joy, love, purpose, hope, and life abundantly, but it does not calm the waves that crash upon the shores of our heart. God will teach us how to surf the waves of life, to overcome in the midst of our circumstances, but the waves will come no matter how good, righteous, and faithful we are (John 16:33). Even Jesus went through the agony of the cross without any special grace from the Father that allowed Him to somehow forego the pain and suffering of dying as a human being. When all else is unclear, the heart of faith simply says, "Into your hands I commit my spirit" (Luke 23:46).

The faith that animates the community of the faithful is less a matter of believing in the existence of God than a practical trust in the person of God, most clearly expressed through His loving care under whatever situation we might find ourselves. In truth, one cannot really say in their heart that, "God exists," until one has said, "I trust you." The first assertion is rational, abstract, a matter of natural theology, the mind laboring with logic to comprehend something greater than itself. The second is based in relationship or communion with a person. Trust may not bring clarity, at least how we understand clarity, but it does bring hope and peace.

Let us return to Grandpa Hansen who was around 87 years old when Mike had the privilege of experiencing this account. Grandpa Hansen had been asked by many if he was bored in his old age. His reply was a firm, "no." Mustering up strength in his voice, he went on to say that he rejoiced in the simplicity of his relationship with Jesus and the good life God had given him. He told Mike that he was grateful for having a radio which afforded him the grand privilege to listen to preachers everyday who expound God's word. Enjoying the moments of life with His heavenly Father as he listened to the declarers of God's mercy and truth provided Grandpa Hansen with rich fuel for his inner man who was being renewed day by day (2 Corinthians 4:16). The simplicity of his life and his gratitude struck Mike profoundly. Grandpa Hansen is purely thankful for all God's blessings upon his life. He had hope because of the person of Jesus and the promise of heaven. As he was awaiting the ultimate fulfillment of his life, going to be with Jesus, Grandpa Hansen drank in each moment, grateful for each breath, radiated love, life, hope, and joy to all who knew him in those last days of his earthly life. As Tom so wonderfully says, Grandpa Hansen was very willing and excited to trade in his body 1.0 for body 2.0, the upgrade. There is something about hope that fosters gratitude and empowers us to live in the middle of promise and fulfillment.

In another conversation Grandpa Hansen and his sister were talking about his dying. She was concerned for him. His reply was an old gospel hymn that contained the lines, "His eye is on the sparrow and I know that He watches me." He relayed his hope in Jesus to her and said he had nothing to be sad about. He would one day go on to be with the Lord (the life in between would then be over). This same confidence was present during lunch when he sang the entire hymn with passion and conviction to Mike and his wife. Grandpa Hansen's hope drove him and gave him a zest for this life because he knew the promise would come to pass. He had something to live for, which gave him a reason to get up each day knowing that one day he would get up (be raised up) one final time for all eternity. Somehow Grandpa

Hansen had found the resolve to life in between, and that answer had a lot to do with the presence of God.

It can then be said that,

> The way of trust is a movement into obscurity, into the undefined, into ambiguity, not into some predetermined, clearly delineated plan for the future. The next step discloses itself only out of a discernment of God acting in the desert of the present moment. The reality of naked trust is the life of a pilgrim who leaves what is nailed down, obvious, and secure, and walks into the unknown without any rational explanation to justify the decision or guarantee the future. Why? Because God has signaled the movement and offered it His presence and His promise. (Manning 12-13)

Are we able to give our lives to God in this manner? Can we trust Him and believe for a better tomorrow? Are we living in a way that tells the world God exists? Is His presence enough for us? Is that the promise we are living for?

The Deceiver's Plan

Life has been described as "the garment we continually alter but which never seems to fit" (McCord). No matter how hard we try, it seems that life either shrinks in the dryer of life or is stretched beyond our capacity to wear it. It is precisely this struggle that heightens our need of control, to find that right elastic, shrink proof fabric that will adjust to the tensions of life. What drives the human heart to question life, itself and God, are struggles, difficulties and pain; each causes us to ask questions about God and life. Listen to the honesty of the characters of the Bible who wrestle with issues very similar to those we have to deal with in the twenty-first century.

> But sir…if the Lord is with us, why has all this happened to us? Where are all his wonders that our fathers told us about when they said, 'Did not the Lord bring us up out of Egypt?' But now the Lord has abandoned us and put us into the hand of Midian. (Judges 6:13 NIV)

> Why is my pain unending

and my wound grievous and incurable?
Will you be to me like a deceptive brook,
like a spring that fails? (Jeremiah 15:18 NIV)

It appears that even without all the spiritual battles we encounter, life, by itself, can be quite hard to fathom. Satan would love to heighten the difficulty of life and living in between the promise and fulfillment by whispering sweet lies about the purpose, person, and plan of God. The enemy would love to have us believe God is either withholding something good from us or simply not noticing us. In layman's language, He has forgotten us. "God is the great neglecting father who quietly bypasses his hurting children" is one of the many effective lies the enemy perpetrates against us.

Satan would love to help confuse you in your journey through pain and struggle: "Your life will never get better"; "You're going to have to take care of yourself because no one will be there to help you"; "You will always be alone"; "It will always be hard." As believers we know God is a present and loving Father. However, in those moments of great trial, the lies of the serpent can be quite persuasive, especially if they speak to our pain and doubt as in the life and journey of Sarai.

Abraham and Sarah

Our story begins with a rather negative and hopeless description of Sarai's barrenness in Genesis 11:30. This situation would be no small problem if you were going to bring many descendents through her. Before we go on, let's describe the situation in detail. We start out with Sarai being barren. Then, God promises to bless Abram and make him into a great nation with many descendants, but his wife is barren. He is *75* years old when this promise comes (Genesis 12:1-4). In Chapter 16 we find Abram, *85* years old, ten years after the promise was given. Sarai decides to help God out with her scheme to have Hagar bear a child for Abram. You know that good old "Plan B" that we so often engage when it looks like God's promise won't work out in the timeframe we had allowed.

In Genesis 17, Abram is *99* years old when the LORD appears to him and promises to increase his numbers. It is here that God changes his name from Abram to Abraham, and Sarai's name to Sarah. Abraham means "father of multitudes" and Sarah means "princess." In Biblical times, the name of the individual represented the person. You could know the person's character simply by their name. To know the name was to know the person (Psalm 9:10). *One's name and existence were closely tied together in Hebrew thought.* Abraham laughs at the possibility of Sarah having a child. Honestly, who wouldn't?

> "...Shall Sarah, who is ninety years old, bear a child?" And Abraham said to God, "Oh that Ishmael might live before you!" God said, "No, but Sarah your wife shall bear you a son, and you shall call his name Isaac... (Genesis 17:17b-19a NIV)

I love God. He simply says, "That's a nice idea Abraham, but I have a plan and I will execute it."

In verses 10-12 of the next chapter in Genesis, three strangers appear and reveal to Abraham that the same time next year they will return and Sarah will be with child. Of course Sarah hears this and bursts into laughter. She responds in sarcasm, "After I am worn out and my master is old, will I now have this pleasure?" (Genesis 18:12 NIV).

Chapter 21 relates God's faithfulness to Sarah -

> Now the Lord was gracious to Sarah as he had said, and the LORD did for Sarah what he had promised. Sarah became pregnant and bore a son to Abraham in his old age at the very time God had promised him...Abraham was a hundred years old when his son Isaac was born to him. (Genesis 21:1-5 NIV)

This is now *25* years after the promise was given.

Then God asked him to sacrifice his only son as a test of his devotion. After all the waiting and the miraculous provision of God for a child, God asks Abraham to sacrifice his future, his dream, and his treasure (Genesis 22:1-2).

It's hard to understand God at times. Most of our Christian life is spent trying to understand His ways. Kosuke Koyama's title of *The Three Mile An Hour God* wonderfully captures the sense of God's speed in our predicaments, rather, our interpretation of how fast He seems to be moving.

What we find in Genesis 16 is a perfect description of what we do in the in between of life. Genesis 16 begins with the painful line, "Now Sarai, Abram's wife, had borne him no children" (1a NIV). This would be bad enough without the previous dialogue between God and Abraham in chapter 15 where Abraham had come to God with the dilemma of being childless. The great patriarch reasoned with God that since he is childless with no provision on the horizon, it would only be expedient that Eliezer be the heir (15:2). Have you ever tried to suggest to God how He should be running your life, particularly when it is not working out like you had thought?

Abram offers Eliezer as the heir. How else can the promise be fulfilled? God declares that Abraham will not have to settle for Eliezer as the heir, but promises in Genesis 15:3 that "a son coming from your own body shall be your heir" (NIV). This implies that Sarai will be the one to bear the child. We remind you, she is not able to bear children, a small problem, the norm of life in between.

What is often not comprehended when reading the Bible is the length of time that has transpired from the word of promise to the current situation we read about. Chapter 16 tells us that 10 years have passed since they settled in Canaan (16:3). That is 10 years since the promise was given; 10 years of rearranging their lives for God with little hope of any promise taking place; 10 years of conversations, arguments, praying, believing, and crying over why it is taking so long.

Sarai's bitterness and need to fix the situation is clearly echoed in her conviction that "The Lord has kept me from having children" (Genesis 16:2 NIV). Not only is she upset with the situation but opts to create a helpful solution to the childless problem. In haste and frustration, she creates a "Plan B" for God's original word and reaffirmed promise in Chapter 15. She opts to use Hagar as the one who would bear the child (16:3). One can hear the quiet frustration between the lines that sounds something like this: "Well, if God isn't going to come through on His promise, I guess I'll have to act and bring it to pass. After all, it's been ten long years of waiting. I can't wait anymore. It's too painful, frustrating, and embarrassing."

The delay after the promise creates a sense of urgency in us. We somehow think we need to act or nothing will come to pass. It is more difficult to wait on another than it is to take matters into one's own hands. M. Basil Pennington, a priest, tells of a time he had breakfast with Mother Teresa of Calcutta. He asked her, "Mother, give me a word of life to bring to my brothers at Spencer [his monastery in Massachusetts]." Mother Teresa looked at him with those penetrating brown eyes, pools of love that invite one to rest in their quiet depths. Finally, she said, slowly and with great emphasis, *"Father, tell them to pray that I do not get in God's way"* (Pennington 35). One has to wonder if the greatest problem we have in between is the struggle with self, a self that inserts itself in God's plan and creates more problems than assistance.

In our Western world it is difficult for us to understand Sarai's plight. In the ancient world, and in some cultures today, it was calamitous for a woman to be without children. The mark of success for a wife was in her great brood of children. Polygamy was often resorted to in the ancient East as a means of obviating childlessness. Wealthy wives - as was Sarai - preferred the option of surrogate motherhood, whereby they allowed their husbands to "go in to" their maids, a euphemism for sexual intercourse (Genesis 6:4; 30:3; 38:8,9; 39:14). The wife could then feel her maid's child was her own and exert some control over it in a way that she could not if her husband had simply taken a second wife.

Abram takes his wife's suggestion and acts on it (the phrase "obeyed his wife" occurs only here and in Genesis 3:17). As is the case in human interactions, tension results and fighting begins with Sarai and Hagar. When Hagar "knew she was pregnant, she began to despise her mistress" (Genesis 16:4b NIV). Sarai is infuriated and filled with jealousy and promptly blames Abram for the problem (16:5 NIV). Now, this might be hard to comprehend in our day and age, but apparently, in the times of the patriarchs wives blamed their husbands for everything.

Abram's passive response, "Your servant is in your hands" is somewhat suspect, particularly since Hagar is now his wife and the mother of his child, and therefore worthy of his protection. We suggest that Abram's soft answer is his attempt to divert her wrath.

As a result of her flagrant attitude, Hagar is treated poorly by Sarai and flees to the wilderness. It is there that she meets the angel of the Lord. When only one angel appears, it must be understood to be God Himself appearing in human form. What a concept: God meets Hagar in her greatest moment of despair. She left Sarai feeling like a nobody with no hope of a tomorrow. God changes all of this. The question of the hour is how?

God meets Hagar in her despair as He will do for us. God does not wait for her. He goes to her: the angel of the Lord found her (Genesis 16:7-8). When God sees, he cares. *She is promised a future for her and her son* (16:10). God gives her hope and personhood. She can be a somebody -- "I am the woman God chose to bless." Ishmael is promised the freedom Hagar sought.

The angel tells her, *"the LORD has heard about your misery"* (16:11 NLT). She is not forgotten. Ishmael means "God hears." Hagar finds her comfort in the presence or person of God. "Thereafter, Hagar referred to the LORD, who had spoken to her, as 'the God who sees me,' for she said, 'I have seen the One who sees me!' Later that well was named Beer-lahairoi ("well of the Living One who sees me.") and it can still be found between Kadesh and Bered" (Genesis 16:13-14 NLT).

What a thought: God sees and hears and will find us in between. If there is anything that brings hope to the human heart, it is the love of God that establishes not only hope, but who we are in Him, which helps us understand who we are in this life.

In Between Shapes Our Destiny

Although we are a society that possesses so much, we seem to be a nation that suffers from the greatest lack. For all we have, it appears we have so little. It would appear that we tend to want what we don't have as Sheryl Crow sings in her 2002 hit song, "Soak Up The Sun": "I don't have digital; I don't have diddly squat; It's not having what you want; It's wanting what you've got" (Interscope Records).

What a paradox this is: to be so affluent and so miserable; to have so much and yet want so much more; to be so wonderfully churched and taught and yet lack the abundant life our Lord said He came to give us; to have received such wonderful promises and yet live most of our lives waiting for them to come to pass. Maybe it would be more accurate to describe "the Land of the Free and the Brave" as "the Land of the Enslaved and Fearful."

What makes this even more of a misery is we have all the things that could make us feel good about ourselves, and yet we still struggle with who we are, not being content and enjoying the now. Like many we are either trapped in our past fearing the future or worried about our future because of our past. Either way, we miss the present moment, allowing our insecurities to flare up and take over, causing destruction and pain along the way.

As believers, this struggle over worth and identity does not end. The tragic irony is that God provides, in His love and kindness, everything we need for our hearts to be at peace with who we are in Him. Perhaps the "in Him" is the problem. Jesus told us that "If a man remains in me and I in him, he will bear much fruit; apart from me you can do nothing" (John 15:5 NIV).

Given the modern familial situation, it is also easy to understand why so many are unable to grasp this concept of God's love. Given the lack of love in families, and parents who are so lost themselves and confused about who they are, many will struggle over their worth. Kids are growing up without the benefit of two parents loving each other and committed to the things of God. Unfortunately, the greatest gift parents could give their children, a stable and loving home environment, is not the norm. *Adding to the pain, parents tend to punish their kids for who they are and not what they've done.* For example, a dad will punish his son or ground him with the words, "You are grounded because you are bad." The distinction between doing bad (action) and being bad (the person as a whole) is blurred. As a result, children grow up sensing they are not worth anything and it is only their acts that matter.

We are not here to discuss the psychological development of children, but to address a larger concern for the church. Many people today have a hard time believing in a God who loves them and thinks well of them. If they do believe at least this, their ideology is warped to the point of simply believing that going to heaven is about being good instead of relationship with God. The implication is "God will love me and let me into heaven because I'm good." What we need to grasp is that God does love us and desires us to be with Him. However, our sin and rebellion have separated us from Him. We can only enter heaven because of God's grace and mercy. The implication here is "God loves me, even though I am sinful, and seeks to restore me to Himself because of His faithfulness to me," or as scripture states, "For Christ died for sins once for all, the righteous for the unrighteous, to bring you to God" (1 Peter 3:18a NIV).

Like the Old Testament figure, Gideon, many today feel rather small, weak, and unable to live as victorious princes and princesses of the King. Rather, we have come to believe that we are of little worth and value to God because we have not been able to live up to our side of the bargain, or that God has abandoned us. The questions demand answers! Where is God when I most need Him? Why hasn't He answered my prayers? Unfortunately, all too many identify with such questions, feeling a sense of cosmic isolation in the vast universe in between.

Life is full of moments when the deepest longings to be loved and appreciated by those we consider important are not satisfied. This is not to say we are not loved or appreciated. Rather, we are simply noting the reality for all of us, and particularly for some, who find such precious commodities missing from their emotional diet. Mike recalls a story of a young man who is able to remember early into his childhood. One of his first memories involves his mother and how she would drop him off at the nursery. He painfully remembers how she would ignore him when she came to pick him up and take him home. He would be crying and yelling for his mom, but she would not come or even look at him. Instead, she would casually talk to the staff and leave him in his misery. He felt invisible and unimportant as these thoughts were seared into his mind, helping shape and form his self-perception. If there is ever a painful moment in life, it can be found in those times of being ignored, abandoned, neglected, passed over, and forgotten.

The Bible does not hide the identity problems of its characters. We come upon a man, whose name is Gideon, in the Old Testament who was simply surviving life, living in fear and anxiety, and living far less than what

God had promised. Gideon poses a question that accurately describes how we feel during those moments of radical loneliness and disillusionment. He despondently replies to the angel of the Lord and asks:

> "But sir," Gideon replied, "if the LORD is with us, why has all this happened to us? Where are all his wonders that our fathers told us about when they said, 'Did not the LORD bring us up out of Egypt?' But now the Lord has abandoned us and put us into the hand of Midian." (Judges 6:13 NIV)

We are not suggesting that we all spin into doubt and despair, nor are we trying to shipwreck your faith. It is true that God is good and works His mysterious will out in our lives. He will complete the work He began. However, it is difficult, when the promise is delayed, to be so sure and live with such strong conviction that it will come to pass.

One of the many reasons we love the Bible is its candid honesty about life and people. Gideon is not portrayed as a dynamic man of faith, but as quite the opposite. He has a sense of cynicism and doubt that drips from his every word. It is precisely people like Gideon that God loves to meet; a man who finds himself living in between with the eyes of his heart focused on his circumstances and his minimal strength and not on the promise giver, God.

If we take a closer look at the book as a whole, we see the problem is not God's negligence, but Israel's sin or need to redefine the relationship. Judges, in chapter two, depicts the scenario quite well.

> After Joshua had dismissed the Israelites, they went to take possession of the land, each to his own inheritance. The people served the LORD throughout the lifetime of Joshua . . . After that . . . They forsook the LORD, the God of their fathers, who had brought them out of Egypt. (2:6-13 NIV)

A careful reading of the book of Judges suggests the conquest was completed, but from the perspective of the book of Judges not all the cities were conquered and many altars were left standing (Judges 2:3; 3:1). From this, we infer the disobedience of Israel was a means that God utilized to bring a deeper understanding of His power and relationship to Israel, revealing that He is faithful to His promise even though the people are not and, when they call upon Him, He will save them.

Judges 6 begins with the unfortunate description, "Again the Israelites did evil in the eyes of the Lord, and for seven years he gave them into the hands of the Midianites" (6:1 NIV). Israel finds herself crying out to God because of the oppression, "Midian so impoverished the Israelites that they cried out to the LORD for help" (Judges 6:6 NIV), and God hears and responds. The devastation to Israel was intense.

> The Midianites were so cruel that the Israelites fled to the mountains, where they made hiding places for themselves in caves and dens. Whenever the Israelites planted their crops, marauders from Midian, Amalek, and the people of the east would attack Israel, camping in the land and destroying crops as far away as Gaza. They left the Israelites with nothing to eat, taking all the sheep, oxen, and donkeys. (6:2-4 NLT)

The attacks were so numerous and the appropriation of the land so flagrant, the people of Israel were left with very little to eat; their sustenance was progressively removed (as is seen in verse 4). This is precisely where we are introduced to Gideon, a man from a small clan and the youngest son of Joash the Abiezrite, who was an idolater. When we are introduced to Gideon we find him threshing wheat in a secret place the Midianites had obviously not discovered.

The call of God upon Gideon is evidence of God's love for His people as He seeks to free them from their sinful turmoil and societal decline. Our faithful God comes on the scene and selects a leader that defies human wisdom and logic. God moves to free His people from bondage and remain faithful to His promise in a way that confounds human understanding.

What makes matters worse is Gideon is no warrior. His clan is not the best suited for such a task. It appears that God not only has the wrong man, but the wrong family. Gideon is well aware of whom he is and responds to the angel, "But Lord...how can I save Israel? My clan is the weakest in Manasseh, and I am the least in my family" (Judges 6:15 NIV). Gideon's response may be true, but it reveals the depth of his insecurity and where his trust is. He is not able to see the situation from the eyes of faith that see a faithful God who is at work in his life. Rather, he views his current state of affairs through the eyes of circumstance and self, causing him to conclude that God has abandoned him and his people.

A lackluster man of faith is Gideon; too real, too broken, with little fight in him. Of all the people God could have selected, He selects this Gideon. One suspects the logic of God's choice.

Gideon's reality was dark and not positive with very little evidence that God was going to do anything in the near future. It is hard to be positive and faithful in times when it seems the walls are closing in. We need no encouragement to see the negative: The human mind has a tendency to view things from a negative perspective. Viewing the glass as half empty or half full is the classic illustration of this. The tragic irony for us as disciples is we have somehow fallen prey to the seduction of the enemy and view the glass as half empty. Our focus is on the circumstance and what is lacking rather than on God and how far we have come. It's time we change our outlook from half empty to half full. To help us to understand our text better, let us tell you a story we created to illustrate our point:

> Once upon a time, there lived a family that had very little; simple survival was difficult, but they managed. The family consisted of a father, a mother, two sons, and a daughter; everything about the family appeared normal.
>
> Normality quickly changed when a band of traveling vagabonds entered the outskirts of town, stopping at the house of this family before entering town. They said they needed a little freshening up. The men barged their way into the house, took food, the women, and left after beating the men.
>
> The father slowly awoke from his unconscious state, only to find the reality far worse than the pain to his person. His heart began to ache over the loss of his wife and daughter. Were they alive? Why God? Why? The questions raced through his mind, as did the emotions. He wavered between tears and rage, faith and doubt.
>
> Suddenly, as if pressed down by some outside force, he fell to his knees and began to weep. Tears rolled from his face as if carrying with each drop a measure of pain that exploded in silent agony onto the floor. The agonizing groan of his soul could be felt in the deepest parts of the night. Heaven wept with him, while Hell mocked in laughter.
>
> The man picked himself up, as if being given a renewed sense of strength, and prayed to God for help. Nothing happened, the heav-

ens were not opened, but the man prayed. One could almost feel the stirring of a quiet wind, a gentle breeze that pulsated with power.

It is almost in this sense of powerlessness that we pick up the story involving Gideon. Things do not look good for the people of Israel and relief is nowhere in sight. What aggravates the situation is the stark reality that the mother and daughter are, for all practical purposes, dead. What is one to do in a time that seems like the dark night of the soul?

God Comes and Gideon Responds

We can see that Gideon is not a man of great courage. He radiates fear and weak faith as the story makes ever so clear. He fears for his life and works under cover. He destroys the Asherah pole at night, not during the day (6:27). He doubts God and needs assurance: He needs a sign, not once, but three times (6:21, 36-40) to help him believe it is God speaking. His faith is weak. He focuses on the situation, the many of the enemy and not the Word of the Lord (7:7). He fears the actual battle (Judges 7:9-15).

One of the major themes in the book of Judges is found in the judges themselves: Whoever is willing to allow God to use them will find that they will be used. It was the dedication of the judges that permitted God to use them, in spite of their far less than exemplary lives - encouragement to us all.

In the midst of being outnumbered, out classed, out everything-ed, caught in the in between of life, it is not surprising that many of us respond like Gideon, "How could you use me?" "How can I get out this situation; I am too messed up to get myself out let alone others?" "But I'm too weak" "My marriage is too far gone to be salvaged!" Like Gideon, our emphasis is on the circumstance and the self and not on the one who can alter life. The clouds are rolling in, and we rightly believe it is going to rain. But maybe, just maybe, the sky will clear.

The Lord promises to be with Gideon, to do his fighting (Judges 6:16), which can only mean victory. One would think Gideon would swell with confidence and shout out in relief. But instead of receiving the promise in faith, Gideon asks for a sign.

God then instructs Gideon to destroy the family and community idols by taking the second best bull from his father's herd, a seven year old, and tearing down his father's altar to Baal and cutting down the Asherah pole near it. Then he is to build an altar to God and use the wood from the Asherah pole to burn the bull as a burnt offering (Judges 6:25-27). Gideon responded to the promise of God like many of us would and needed a little more assurance that the promise was real. Gideon eventually believed the promise but what followed this faith was not what one would expect. Gideon proceeds to obey God but does so in timidity and fear. Gideon may have believed in God's promise to remove the bondage (the Midianites), but he still believed that his life might be lost if he really trusted God (Judges 6:29-30). Apparently, there were real consequences for his obedience, as is often the case for those in between. For Gideon finds himself not only in between the promise and the fulfillment but in between faith and doubt. Be encouraged. It is this man God selects. There is hope for us all.

Many believers find themselves in a situation like Gideon's. They hide and live in fear, trying to eke out an existence while they hope anxiously that the little life they have found is not taken away. As a result, many live their lives with one eye fixed on their little hidden treasure and the other on losing it. The following are some principles from the story of Gideon that might instill some hope.

First, God is attentive to our cries and our condition (Judges 6:6-7). Living in between as we do, we often wonder if God even ever hears us. He does, and He responds, just as He did to Gideon.

God will bring deliverance through a life that is obedient (Judges 6:14). "Am I not sending you?" The language is that of covenant, "You go and I will supply." More simply, as you step out in faith, God will supply the power and strength to go on.

We must remove our idols and their altars (Judges 6:25-32). The first thing Gideon is asked to do is remove the altars, and that is the first task on our journey with the Lord, getting rid of those high places of worship in our lives, those things we place in priority before God.

Trust God, He will come through, "When the three hundred trumpets sounded, the LORD caused the men throughout the camp to turn on each other with their swords" (Judges 7:22a NIV). The plan of attack that God chose to employ involved very few of the original 32,000 men with Gideon (7:3). God wants Gideon to fight the battle His way (7:2; 7:7). God even addresses Gideon's fear by saying, "If you are afraid to attack, go down to the camp with your servant Purah and listen to what they are saying. Afterward, you will be encouraged to attack the camp" (7:10-11a NIV). Gideon goes down and hears the man expressing a dream involving a round loaf of barley bread which came tumbling into the Midianite camp and struck the tent with such force that it knocked it over (7:13-15). That was all Gideon needed.

To trust Christ is to put first His kingdom. Do so and you will see the power of the Almighty at work in your life! The Lord has come to you in your life and is saying: "The Lord is with you, mighty warrior." How will you respond?

Praise: The Barometer of Faith and Trust

Mustering up a joyful shout of praise or even finding it within yourself to softly say "thank you, God" is increasingly difficult in the in between of life. It is hard to trust this God who at the moment does not appear to be all that kind and caring, because the promise made is nowhere near fulfillment and your life, well, that's another story.

The Old Testament prophet Habakkuk helps us on our journey here. The book starts with the complaint of the prophet as he is trying to find understanding for the injustice around him:

> How long, O LORD, must I call for help? But you do not listen! "Violence!" I cry, but you do not come to save. Must I forever see this sin and misery all around me? Wherever I look, I see destruction and violence. I am surrounded by people who love to argue and fight. The law has become paralyzed and useless, and there is no justice given in the courts. The wicked far outnumber the righteous, and justice is perverted with bribes and trickery. (Habakkuk 1:2-4 NLT)

What we glean from the dialogue between Habakkuk and God is the prophet's desire to enter in conversation with God. He not only asks the questions, but waits around for a reply. He challenges God with questions but does so with a heart of submission, one that is in relationship with God. Habakkuk expects God to reply and does not intend to turn his heart away from Him. He is willing to declare his ignorance and confusion over the ways of God and even asks the Holy One, "What's up?" But all of this is done in a posture of reverence.

The prophet is somehow able to break out into praise after being in the presence of the Lord and sharing the frustration of his heart. The prophet's heart, in spite of his confusion, is bent in submission to God's greatness. There is something about praise that signals death to the self and releases life, giving birth to hope.

Maybe the issue at stake is our willingness to let God govern the world and, more importantly, our lives. Growth in Christ can only come by death to ourselves, hope in Him, faith in His character, and self-denial. Let us turn to the Francois Fenelon, Archbishop of Cambrai, France during the seventeenth century, who writes these poignant and instructive words about dying to the self:

> I am aware that it is the life of self which causes us pain; that which is dead does not suffer. If we were really dead, and our life hid with Christ in God (Colossians 3:3), we would no longer struggle with those pains in spirit that now afflict us...We can add to our God-given cross by agitated resistance and an unwillingness to suffer. This is simply evidence of the remaining life of self. (2-3)

What the life in between definitely reveals is what is most alive in us and where our treasure really lies. Maybe it is the greater injustice that we who profess the Holy Name of God are really no different from anyone else? We are just as anxious, fearful, angry, divorced, judgmental, etc., as those who do not have the hope of Jesus. This is precisely the place many need to begin.

Some of us cry out for the blessing of God, a better life, a life of minimal pain and suffering. Maybe the problem is less God's supposed inaction then our unwillingness to recognize God as the only true source of joy (Deuteronomy 8:3). Like Gideon we have settled for lives far less than what God created us for and exist in fear and anxiety, coming to believe that the in between of life is permanent. Larry Crabb offers this insightful comment:

> In all of it, the point of things seems to be us, not God. How we're getting along at any moment seems more important than whether we're connecting with God. And when we do think about connecting with God, we tend to be more concerned with what's in it for us than with finding real power and clearer vision so we can better further His purposes." (Crabb, *Cry of the Soul*, Foreword 9)

Henry Van Dyke has said it well: "Self is the only prison that can bind the soul." There is nothing more binding than the prison of the self. Far too many spend too much time in this self made prison. The Greek myth of Narcissus illustrates how the prison of the self leads to nothing but isolation, despair, and pain. The Greek hero was a beautiful specimen of a man, who, in his arrogance, would not consent to being loved by others. In so doing, he found himself cursed one day by one of the nymphs. The curse was a reflection of his life; as he had not returned love when loved, may he find love in life but not be able to experience it.

One day when washing in a river, he was overcome by the face in the water. His own image had pierced his heart unknowingly and he fell in love with himself. He smiled at the image and it returned the smile. He gazed in deep admiration and it returned the gaze of fondness. As he reached out to embrace the image it broke up in the water. Narcissus was overcome with inexpressible pain as he tried to understand why the image, who was returning love, would not allow for an embrace. And so, in misery Narcissus lived in bondage to himself. May God free us from our self made prisons!

Living in between as we do, it is all too easy to fall into the traps of self. To keep us out of these self-made incarcerations, we must point our focus and hope to the future Kingdom, walking in the in between with patient endurance.

CHAPTER FIVE

The Riddle of Life: "Confused and Confusing"

Rick Chollet had it all. The son of struggling French immigrants, he started a company called Brookstone, a small mail-order tool business, which found itself as a successful national purveyor of unique gadgets. Not only was he riding high on the wave of corporate achievement and notoriety, he was handsome, happily married, and loved by his employees and colleagues. In spite of owning the so-called perfect life, Chollet was despondent. On March 18 of 1991, he took his life. "Please forgive me, but the thought of going through the torture of living is just too much to bear" was the note he left for his family just before locking the garage door of his New Hampshire house and climbing into his BMW and turning on the engine. His wife, Susan, stated that Chollet had been depressed for most of his adult life. The pressure of being put on a pedestal, coupled with the anxiety of letting the people down was too much for him to bear. "He swung from feeling totally powerful to totally helpless" (Gelman and Friday 56).

The feeling of helplessness is a strange and terrifying state in which to find oneself. It's not just the male populace that struggles with such a foe. Women are caught in the rat race of having to be beautiful and successful, feminine and aggressive. All too often, the woman finds herself dressing with social confidence, looking to her body to attract the attention she wants, but crying out within to be loved for who she is. A sense of feeling trapped in a world of external beauty and performance dominates the interior world of many women. If nothing else, is there not a sense of anxiety that comes about every time you notice the enemy of age setting in? Our culture demands so much from women when it comes to beauty. It is as if she is less valued when the mystique of beauty wears off. A paradox of dynamic proportions exists as we are socialized to think a man who ages and loses his youthful physique becomes distinguished and a woman who does the same just becomes old. To compete and find acceptance in such a cold world, the woman finds herself feeling like she must fit the *Cosmopolitan* ideal and be something other than human. As many feel, to be accepted for being beautiful, or for one's intelligence, is somewhat painful; deep within sits the agonizing feeling of not being acknowledged for being yourself. The fear of losing the beauty or having someone with greater intelligence replace us is very real. Risking oversimplification, the state of helplessness, of feeling trapped by life, might be more common than we care to admit. Compounding the fear is the pressure to become somebody, to make something of oneself; resulting in tragic endings like Chollet's, "self-handicapping" behaviors (blames the failure on something other than the person's own incompetence), and/or sheer internal dissatisfaction with life.

To admit that life is frustrating and not what we expect is absolutely depressing. Growing old causes us to face our finiteness, as the quiet lack in life thrusts us forward into the real world wherein very few people like to live. Life in between only exacerbates the problem making ever so clear that life and God are not bringing us what we thought they would.

When was the last time you found yourself questioning existence? "Is this all there is?" "Who am I?" "What am I about?" "Will I ever make it?" "Does anybody care?" "Has my life made a difference?" "Is God real?" "Does God care?" "Why do I have to live so much of life in this state of in between?" These questions I'm sure we've all asked ourselves at some point in our lives. This interrogation of existence along with the constant throb of loneliness or inadequacy is found in the heart of many lives, pounding to the rhythm of fear. There are many questions, and often, not enough answers. Life is a confusing set of decisions, the pursuit of which often leaves us uncertain.

If you like security and are seeking to find it, we have bad news for you: Nothing seems permanent anymore. The irony of life is the permanence of death and insecurity. We can safely say that what is secure is the constant quest for security and the disillusionment many feel as they come up empty handed. For example, some marriages may be nothing more than temporary arrangements wherein each partner politely uses the other to find happiness. When the so-called magic wears off, a newer model is sought to fill the internal gap. Many relationships end up resembling a rather tragic scenario of two ticks with no dog. Each partner looks to the other for life and happiness and blames the other when it does not occur. The "white picket fence" dream has turned into a painful nightmare or even worse, a boring dream.

The nuclear family is almost extinct. Stability in the familial structure is no longer a part of practical living. If you find yourself living in a large metropolitan area, you have undoubtedly discovered it's not normal to call up grandma to babysit the kids or even call mom to do so. If the family is in the area they are often too far away or too busy to help. Families, for the most part, do not live near each other, nor do many families seem to cherish the ritual of family gatherings as once they did. Holidays are intensely stressful for many young married couples who have to decide which set of parents to visit, and deciding which of the divorced parents should be visited. No wonder so many people are in therapy, support groups and various self-help seminars, seeking harmony and self-fulfillment in various religions, turning to drugs and alcohol, and taking their own lives.

Society has turned into one large fragment of human existence, where life is not truly experienced but simply acknowledged. Life has been reduced to a compartmentalized segment, where the soul is asked to divide itself between the working self and the fun and free self. We are no longer one solid self, but a variety of selves with no comprehension on what ties the differing roles together. Internal torment is common to all lives as we attempt to figure how to keep the varying roles cohesive. Discovering the answer to the perennial question of "who am I?" is nearly impossible in our fragmented society. Individuals are too divided to know how to define themselves and too confused over the soul's internal longing for a greater something. A thirst of huge proportions drives the weary human soul to look for something to quench the divided self.

In *Mega Trends 2000*, David Naisbitt and Patricia Aburdene make an informed prediction about the 21st century. "The most exciting breakthroughs of the 21st century will occur not because of technology but because of an expanding concept of what it means to be human" (16). They add, "Science and technology do not tell us what life means. We learn that through literature, the arts and spirituality" (272). The question that will need to be answered will involve human existence and meaning. In essence, "What is life about?" What people seem to be after today is meaning and self-fulfillment. You may ask, what's new about that?

It's obvious the quest for meaning is not new. The irony to the quest is our inability to find life no matter how hard we pursue it. With all the massive technology and brilliance we possess today, humanity is not one step closer to self-definition. As a matter of fact, we may be more disillusioned...but don't tell anybody. This leads to even more confusion.

> You've got enough insights to last you three hundred years. The most urgent need in your life is to trust what you have received...Of what avail is our life of prayer, our study of scripture, theology, and spirituality, if we do not trust the insights that we have received. Waffling back and forth between a decisive "yes" and a discouraging "no" keeps us in a state of terminal procrastination. (Manning 1)

The answer many turn to in such a situation is God. The church responds "give all to Jesus and life will be better." Pain is quickly addressed and brushed aside with the victory message of the cross as the soldiers of the militant army of denial march in rhythm to the drum beat of make believe. "Christ experienced radical shame, pain, rejection, poverty and death so we wouldn't" the religious community professes with the utmost confidence. As true as the latter statement might be, is it correctly understood and applied?

The church appears to be busy in its mission to save lives from this world, at face value a worthy and righteous endeavor. But in its evangelistic zeal, it seems the church has somehow missed the mark. Jesus became a man, walked among people and participated in human existence. He became the model for life and was life itself. The church, on the other hand, wants people to step out of life into a fabricated world of mythical bliss, where the hero never dies and the villain is always destroyed. But is justice really that black and white for the Christian in the here and now? Listen to the words of Asaph:

> Truly God is good to the upright, to those who are pure in heart. But as for me, my feet had almost stumbled, my steps had well nigh slipped. For I was envious of the arrogant, when I saw the prosperity of the wicked. For they have no pangs; their bodies are sound and sleek. They are not in trouble as other men are; they are not stricken like other men. Therefore pride is their necklace; violence covers them as a garment. Their eyes swell out with fatness, their hearts overflow with follies. They scoff and speak with malice; loftily they threaten oppression. They set their mouths against the heavens, and their tongue struts through the earth. Therefore the people turn and praise them; and find no fault in them. And they say, "How can God know? Is there knowledge in the Most High?" Behold,

> these are the wicked; always at ease, they increase in riches. All in vain have I kept my heart clean and washed my hands in innocence. For all the day long I have been stricken, and chastened every morning. (Psalm 73:1-14 RSV)

Reality is difficult to embrace. The pain of our yesterdays combined with the agony of the present is all too often too much to bear. Then there is the general meaningless confusion of it all. In such a setting, Jesus becomes an easy way out of life. But is this the type of life scripture calls us to live? Maybe this is precisely why any sane human being seeks to withdraw from life. Pain, despair and confusion are fantastic motivators to create a system of relief where denial is the dominant thrust. If anything will drive people to find a solution to the dilemma, it is the desire for relief from pain. Christ is the ultimate source of relief from the pain of life and is often pursued as a way to deny the reality of common existence. Is Jesus supposed to be a scapegoat? A method of denial? Are we supposed to deny life to find it? Or do we find life and then deny it?

Reality dictates that Christians are not immune to suffering. Christians feel the sting of pain, deal with the questions of existence, and the fear of being exposed for who they really are. All too often the believer is set up for a trap where real life has to be denied and false religious joy and happiness lived out. The plastic answers and scathing rebukes when pain and doubt are confessed only encourage the frightened and confused believer to live in the world of fabricated joy. Thus, the internal world is denied existence and gently asked to hide. Anxiety becomes the common state for such a person who worries about being found out. Coupled with anxiety are two old friends for many, guilt and shame, the feeling like one is an absolute failure as a believer because of not being able to live the holy life like everyone else is doing. As a result, true feelings and humanness are strategically denied and hidden within an exterior of righteous behavior and sugar-coated joy. Dietrich Bonhoeffer makes a rather interesting point:

> The pious fellowship permits no one to be a sinner. So everybody must conceal his sin from himself and from the fellowship. We dare not be sinners. Many Christians are unthinkably horrified when a real sinner is suddenly discovered among the righteous. So we remain alone with our sin, living in lies and hypocrisy. (*Life Together* 110)

The strange reality of church life is when people are asked to be something other than human, to attend the gathering of those who are celebrating the joy of living life. All are requested to be happy and well-adjusted, to smile and portray the American ideal of the happy individual, to leave real life at home, to pretend all is well when all is not. You may fool the world, but it's difficult to fool yourself. If there is a voice which haunts us at night, it is the one quietly whispering in our dark chambers of despair reminding us that all is not well in the land of "blessed assurance." No wonder discord or inner tension is so prominent in the lives of so many Christians. It takes a tremendous amount of work to live two lives.

So what does a Christian do when despair is felt? How does one deal with life in Christ when it isn't all it's said to be? Where does one turn if the Jesus connection isn't working?

The Reality of Despair

Happiness is analogous to the wind. We feel its effects, but cannot grasp it. It's one of those commodities we work hard to find only to realize the climb over the mountain is less than we expected. For some it's not at all what was expected. Have you ever noticed that the joy of acquiring a new home or car quickly evaporates? Deep inside, a sense that something is still missing rises softly in our soul. As wonderful as the house might be, it still lacks that extra something our hearts long to find.

Many people look to the arena of relationships for the answer to the dull ache of emptiness in their hearts. The thrill of being loved and having a beautiful woman or handsome man next to you is definitely a boost to one's sense of identity, and quietly calms the storm of loneliness for the moment. To be loved and cared for thrusts the ego into the land of identity and internal bliss for a season of inexpressible joy. However, if you are internally desperate and lonely before marriage, chances are quite high you will be after as well. The short lived relief we experience in relationship is nothing more than a pain-killer that alleviates the intensity of the ache but does nothing for the problem. The symptom is treated while the cause is ignored. Eventually we wake up from the dream and realize the knight in shining armor or the beautiful princess was nothing more than an image on the movie screen of our minds. Too often the theater of imagination is more real than life itself as it replays our favorite movies over and over of what we believe life will be like when the majestic man or angelic woman walks on the scene. The motto goes something like, "Life will begin for me, when..." What is your "when?" What are you waiting for that will make life really full and enjoyable for you?

Maybe we can illustrate our point with the following story by David Reynolds called, "Stoptime."

Little Suzy was in kindergarten. One day she brought home a pumpkin seed from class. Her homework assignment was to plant the seed and water it and grow a pumpkin for next Halloween. She packed rich, black soil into a glass jar, planted her seed, watered it carefully, and set it on the kitchen window shelf. Then she sat down to watch the seed grow.

"What are you doing, Suzy?" her teen-aged sister, Lucy, asked.

"I'm waiting for the pumpkin to grow so that I can put it in a larger jar," Suzy replied.

"Silly," Lucy laughed. "It will take a long time before that pumpkin comes up."

"That's all right; I'll wait. What are you doing sitting by the phone?"

"I'm hoping Bill will call me. He's that cute new guy at school. I think he likes me."

"Does he know our phone number?" Suzy asked a sensible question.

"Hmmm. Maybe. He knows Bob, and Bob knows it."

"Oh."

Just then their father entered the kitchen.

"Any telephone calls for me, Lucy?" he asked.

"No, not this morning. Anything special?"

"Well, I sent that manuscript off to the publisher's last week. They should let me know soon if they want to handle it or not."

"Well, nothing so far."

"Thanks, I'd better get back to that lawnmower." He grabbed a can of beer from the refrigerator and went back out through the screen door.

From the next room Lucy's mother's voice could barely be heard above the whir of the sewing machine. She was talking to herself. "When will that man come to his senses about the writing business? He could be making a good, steady living as an engineer. I've waited sixteen years for the light to dawn on him that he'll never make it as an author. If it weren't for my sewing and his parents' money..."

The cat scratched at the screen door. Suzy ran to let it in. Tail in the air, her chubby pet headed for the cupboard where the cat food was kept. It sat and scratched and whined in its cat's voice, waiting to be fed.

This story seems to be getting nowhere, the author thought.
Perhaps tomorrow I'll think of an inspiring ending. (138-139)

In this story everyone is waiting for something: Suzy is waiting for the pumpkin seed to grow; Lucy is waiting for a telephone call; the cat is waiting to be fed; even the author is waiting to finish the story. Some people seem to turn their lives off as they wait for something, which is precisely what happens for the believer living in between. There are countless numbers of people who only wait and do not use their time wisely while waiting. For Mike's oldest daughter (who is five at the time of writing), what does she do when she is waiting for her turn in a game, when she is waiting in line at Disneyland for the next thrill ride, or when she is waiting for her friend next door to come out and play? Life seems very long to young people, but it is too short to waste even a minute. Young or old, we recommend that you fill your waiting moments with life, trusting God with details, and enjoying the day you have. Believe it or not, you can live in between and still enjoy life. The moral of our story is, "Don't put your life on hold."

What are you waiting for in life? Is life passing you by as you wait for that something to happen before you are really able to begin to live? Do you find yourself in despair because you feel inside that it (life) will never really happen for you? Are you afraid to venture out for fear that somehow the little ownership you have of life will be stripped?

Despair is such a common element in human life. If for nothing else, we feel tension in that we desire to be known and fear it at the same time. Have you ever noticed how strongly you desire connection with people, but fear becoming too close? Maybe you find yourself wanting to trust people but are afraid to do so, wanting desperately to be understood but experiencing misunderstanding every time you attempt to connect with others. To adequately deal with despair, we will often seek to cover it with a blanket of busyness. Many live in the world of unrealistic accomplishment in the pursuit of unattainable goals. If we can keep our minds on something else maybe the nagging reality of despair will disappear. Well, there is nothing like denial to help us cope with life.

The world of entertainment and week-end living is an indicator of the internal boredom, meaninglessness, and despair many feel and seek to avoid. The drive to withdraw from reality is a common factor in the arena of life. We withdraw to deal with the painful and harsh emptiness of being alive. Maybe that's why the world will spend millions of dollars on entertainment. We look to the movie stars for hope and a promise of a better tomorrow. *Terminator 2*, the 1990's sci-fi thriller about the destructive tendency of human nature, provides a dose of encouragement and hope for all who are concerned about the self-destructive nature of people. The movie revolves around the theme of destruction. Humanity is set on a course to destroy itself and will if not stopped. As a matter of fact, Arnold Schwarzenegger's character, T-800, now the good terminator (a paradox in itself), says a rather powerful and telling statement. The scene is set at a country gas station. The good Terminator is working on the car and the young boy, John, is talking with him. The conversation is interrupted by two little boys who are playing with plastic guns and pretending to shoot each other. The camera action slows the movements of the two boys down as the violence of the two little kids picks up. John says: "We aren't going to make it, are we?" Schwarzenegger's character responds: "No, it's in your nature to destroy yourselves."

The movie goes on to paint a graphic picture of the hopeless state we are in and the course of doom we are on. "No fate but that which we make" becomes the catch all theme of the movie. Our future can be created in the now, our destinies fixed today. The future is considered to be something that is not set in stone, but a variable that can be adjusted by actions in the present. As true as this might be, can we really change our destiny by a simple shift of our structure or an adjustment of the external world? Will the simple removal of evil from society provide for a richer and peaceful life?

Frederick Buechner describes the human predicament with blatant honesty:

> The truth, for instance, that left to ourselves, as a race we are doomed - what else can we conclude? Doomed if only by our own insatiable lust for doom. Despair and destruction and death are the ancient enemies, and yet we are always so helplessly drawn to them that it is as if we are more than half in love with our enemies. Even our noblest impulses and purest dreams get all tangled up with them just as in Vietnam, in the name of human dignity and freedom, the bombs are falling on both the just and the unjust and we recoil at the horror of little children with their faces burned off, except that somehow that is the way the world has always been and is, with nightmare and noble dream all tangled up together. That is the way we are doomed - doomed to be what we are, doomed to seek our own doom. And the turbulent waters of chaos and nightmare are always threatening to burst forth and flood the earth. We hardly need the tale of Noah to tell us that. The New York Times tells us

> just as well, and our own hearts tell us well too, because chaos and nightmare have their little days there also. (*The Hungering Dark* 41)

The answer to our dilemma is not found in a simple shift in our activities, a progressive attempt by humanity, as good as it would be, to better our living conditions and our world. Something far deeper must take place before anything promising can occur which will have lasting effects for the entire human race as opposed to a slight benefit for a few. Professor Jerome Murphy-O'Connor adds this insightful comment:

> Oppressive structures will not be successfully modified until hearts are changed. It is true that human beings change as new structures emerge, but the consistent lesson of history is that without genuine conversion the new structures will prove to be no less oppressive. (10)

The trust in human goodness and the ability to solve our plight is slowly waning; the world wars and constant tension between nations today loudly voices the distressing news that the world problem is a personal one. Nations are nothing more than human personality made corporate. Like two siblings fighting over a place of importance and favor with dad, nations wrestle over matters of politics, land, religion, oil, etc. At the heart of our political and international crisis are hearts that have been offended, misunderstood, betrayed, etc. The difference now is that little brother does not simply hit his big brother or pull away and ignore him, little brother can order an air assault, withhold food and rations, increase taxes, and even murder in the name of a god.

Can we simply solve the problem by encouraging people to become active in the social and political arena? The logic is simple, but profound: If all become like the Good Samaritan of Luke's gospel, the world would become a better place. Obviously engaging in the affairs of human existence is a positive step towards social change and even necessary. But is it enough? Whose social and political agenda are we suppose to follow? Naturally, everyone would like the world to be the way they believe it should be. So, whose world view is the proper one to employ for the betterment of society?

With everyone professing, in essence, to be the center of life, that is understanding life through one's own personal agenda, it is no wonder chaos and tension exist between people. To give place to a relative world view that says "whatever works for you is fine" is to advance the problem.

Accommodating others with this so-called advanced and accepting philosophy is really nothing more than securing your own personal island of life with a strong sense of "don't tell me how to live my life and I won't tell you how to live yours." What a strange philosophy, to advocate the terrible tragedy of disconnectedness and human isolation. As we secure the rule of the self on our individual islands of life, we do nothing more than water the plant of selfish living that seeks to love only those who come into our little worlds of Eden on our terms. In other words, "come into my world only as I permit." The problem is we are more than individuals: We are community whether we like it or not. Understanding the nature of being community is not all that fearful for some as long as the mechanism of control is in their hands. If we have community, the inference is "come on over to my house and I'll tell you how our wonderful, little community will function."

If people live on guarded islands, accepting contact only when beneficial, then how do we work on a national or international level to solve the problems our world faces? The problems of the environment, AIDS, identity and a host of other issues are pressing us for resolution. The solution necessary for global change involves the person, but enforcing a mode for personal change acceptable for the world at large is a trifle difficult. Whose fault is it that "Mother Earth" and human nature have ended up in this awful predicament of gradual depletion of our natural resources? Is it the rich who have no concern for the poor? Is it America as it disregards the rest of the world in its blatant use of the Earth's natural resources? Is it the government that is at fault? Maybe the fault is more personal than we care to admit. If we do agree that it is personal, we opt out of any responsibility by arguing that it is the personal problem of our neighbor, not us, because we have already given at the office.

With such a desperate situation about us, no wonder most live out a shadowy existence during the work week only to come alive at the weekend in the land of pleasure. If we, by chance, live in suburbia, we encounter other factors: busyness and disconnectedness. The corporate executive or hard working laborer is left with a sense of lack after the work week and finds himself longing for some kind of human connection when the weekend hits.

There must be more to life than working all week, having fun on the weekends, and taking that family vacation every year. After all this, have you ever found yourself feeling less than fulfilled, saying "the time away was great but...", the soul whispering, "Is this all there is to life?" If there is ever a time to quiet the whisper, it is in those moments of stark honesty. Busyness or success or a movie can do wonders for burying the truth of life and sprinkling our disillusioned hearts with hope and temporary sanity. The adage that "reality is the leading cause of stress" is not far from the truth.

It is precisely the question of "Is this all there is?" that many male corporate executives are asking themselves. Having achieved his dreams and financial desires, the male executive finds himself feeling unfulfilled. "Is this it?" is the question many ask. "OK, I've accomplished a lot in my life, but so what!"

Life is an interesting phenomenon. We live it like there is nothing wrong. All of our attempts to better humanity, as worthy as they might be, leave a lot to be desired. No matter how hard we try the world moves closer to darkness and despair. With all the sophistication we possess, we still can't figure out how to establish peace in the world nor peace within ourselves. The reality of darkness in our world is more real than we care to admit. Darkness is the primary theme of our news broadcasts, literature, and movies. Our private lives are full of the gnawing menace as well. If we are people who are apt to pray, darkness is probably what a majority of our prayers are about. If we are people who no longer pray, it's probably because in one way or another, our mouths have been stopped cold with darkness. It is the cosmic darkness that tends to overshadow the light of hope in between.

It is as if the very fabric of humanity is laced with despair. The thread of self-destruction lines the human fabric. The equation is absolutely terrifying:

Knowledge + Sophistication = Despair + Anxiety

How much easier has life really become with all the advancements we have made? Are you less stressed since the creation of all of our high-tech gadgets? How much more rested do you feel because of the time you save cooking with the microwave? Maybe our problem is we are trying to cram too much into life to fill the vacuum within. The more we try to define our existence the more frustrated we become. Maybe life is not meant to be found inside, but outside of life. The radical mystery of our modern times is that we can describe life but cannot find it; we can even busy ourselves in life, but are unable to locate it in the midst of ever increasing activities. "Life, where art thou?"

CHAPTER SIX

The Riddle of Humanity: "Embracing Ambiguity, Gaining Clarity"

Lost Without a Map

Have you wondered which way is up or down, been confused as to the direction you need to go? Of course, if you are a typical male, if you'll permit us to stereotype the masculine nature (and the authors are guys!), you would probably never admit you don't know where you are going, and certainly never admit to being lost. There is something strange in the male psyche that has an aversion to stopping at the local gas station to ask the attendant for directions. The challenge of finding the place on his own, coupled with the humiliation of being lost moves the man to locate the desired destination by himself. Success without any outside aid is the primary focus of the mission as we seek to conquer the map and the skeptical voices which challenge our map working ability. If you don't succeed, and fail to find the place, may your wife be one who is prone to grace and gentleness as you sheepishly make your way to the gas station for directions and humbly admit defeat. Enough rambling, the point we wish to make is *we all have at one time or another felt the awfulness of being lost.* Maybe this is precisely the problem with our human existence. We are lost, and living in between only makes that ever so clear.

What does it mean to be human? This is no doubt the place where the passionate interest of the inquiring mind and the divine message of scripture meet and come into conflict. Basically, humanity regards itself as the center of life and of this world. Of course, we acknowledge the vastness of the universe and our infinitesimal size in relation to it, but still live as though we are the center, the driving force of this existence. With each person professing to be his/her own center, chaos results and disintegration of the human race continues. To ask the question about human existence is to begin a process where life can no longer be taken for granted. In asking the question we find just how much we lack the ability to answer it adequately or satisfactorily. The questioning of our existence challenges our surroundings, the shell of our livelihood. As we find our surroundings challenged, an insecurity of incredible magnitude begins to make itself known. There is a whole lot to this life that seems to be, at least on the surface, vague and ambiguous. Life is a riddle that plagues the intelligence of our most sophisticated minds by posing questions the brilliant are unable to answer with any degree of certainty. Mind you, this is not to imply that people are not certain of their answers, but to suggest the lack of certainty in the answer proclaimed. Complicating the dilemma, we must add that not only is the world full of riddles, but the one who asks the questions is also a riddle. How can we solve the riddle of life if we cannot solve the riddle of the human state which lives in internal contradiction?

The nature of the beast is precisely contradiction -- humanity lives in internal contradiction. It is this internal contradiction that leads us to our disorientation, our lostness. What a thought! Deep within the human psyche we find dissonance that resonates in soft tones, whispering for relief and harmony. This longing for fulfillment and relief in life creates a rather disturbing tendency in modern humanity; we answer the whisper for relief by denying its existence.

> The human being who knows nothing about his human existence, and does not inquire into it, is not a human being; this existence freed from all questioning is not human but animal existence, and those who consider this to be the correct view would do well not to write clever books about 'the mind as the enemy of the soul.' (Brunner 30)

We bury the beast deep within the soil of denial. The chaos of life is ignored and simply organized into nice and tidy systems of thought or created realities of external bliss; much like an executive who has piles of paperwork on his desk takes the chaotic work which demands his attention and sorts it into ordered piles. The chaos still exists: The ambiguity of life still resounds in our mental ears, but now sits in decorative fashion relieving the frustrated tension of the hard working executive. At least now he knows where things are. The human race finds a sense of relief in being able to place things into certain piles. We seek to define things and categorize them in an effort to understand them. To put things in such nice boxes, to define them, means we must have control over them. That sense of definition and control eases the stress our souls feel from the chaos around us. Unfortunately, the reality is we do not control a great many of the stress-inducers of life, but rather live under the self-inflicted spell of such an illusion.

Many deal with the reality of internal contradiction like a little kid who has been asked to clean his room. Craftily and quickly, the child scurries about his room cleaning and re-arranging the mess. To avoid really dealing with the mess that exists, the child takes everything and puts it under the bed; again the chaos is organized and this time completely out of one's constant view. The non-observant mother or father comes in and inspects the room with pleasure and applauds the child's efforts. Maybe the latter is the more popular mode people take. The neater and tidier we make or hide our piles, the more the world rejoices at the ingenuity of the creative mind to organize the chaos. There is nothing like denial for tying the human race together in the effort of burying the beast within. Listen to the powerful and poignant words of Scott Peck: "We attempt to skirt around problems rather than meet them head on. We attempt to get out of them rather than suffer through them" (16). He goes on to say: "This tendency to avoid problems and the emotional suffering inherent in them is the primary basis for all human illness." (17) "Neurosis is always a substitute for legitimate suffering," adds Carl Jung (quoted in Peck 17).

Maybe the first of "The Four Noble Truths" of Buddhist teaching is more accurate than we care to admit as it declares, "Life is suffering." Jesus said it this way: "...In this world you will have trouble..." (John 16:33 NIV) Oh, now there is a joyous thought for you to digest, one that becomes ever so apparent on the road in between.

So, how much stuff have you attempted to place under your bed? Is your system able to adequately hold the confusion of life and cover up the quiet lack and dissonance ringing within? Do you get nervous when people get close to your bed and might actually look underneath, and really see you for who you are?

The more brilliant the scheme of organization, the more tension is created; only so much stuff will fit underneath one's bed. The creative genius of today allows us the ability to make larger beds and decorate the room to comfort the eye and alleviate our pain for a season. However, no matter how hard we try to stabilize chaotic life, we are constantly forced back into reality every time we have to lay our heads on the pillow at night. There we are met with ravaging questions of doubt, the nagging hunger for something more, and feelings of insecurity. It's almost as if the chaos floats to the surface when we are alone, reminding us that all is not well in our land of make believe. An insightful description of the human plight is found in the writings of Brunner. He writes:

> Man is not at home with himself; as he is, he cannot come to terms with himself. He desires to be and to express himself as that which he is; yet at the same time he does not want to be what he is. Hence he conceals himself behind his ideals. He is ashamed of his naked existence as it is. He cannot tolerate it; he feels that in some way or other he must live for a future existence in order to endure his own view of himself. If some way or other he counts the 'higher' element as his, in order to be able to say 'yes' to himself, and yet he knows that this 'higher' element is not real. (Brunner 20-21)

Like Neo in the movie, *The Matrix*, we know there is something wrong, "a splinter in the mind," and yet we do not know how to get ourselves out of the confines of the matrix. We live our lives believing that what we see is real and all there is, coupled with the splinter in our minds that alludes to the possibility that there is something wrong.

The human is thus divided inside and knows this to be so, suffering accordingly, and, on account of this very contradiction, attempts to be freed from the confines of the matrix. And yet, can freedom within the matrix actually be true freedom? The success of such endeavors has been somewhat limited. Freedom has turned into nothing more than managed bondage. If we can convince ourselves that we are truly free then maybe we will really live life and everything will be ok.

If humanity is the riddle, then how does the riddle resolve the riddle?

Afraid of Mirrors

People, particularly women, struggle with the stark reality a mirror portrays about the human body. There is, often, nothing more depressing than looking into a mirror and seeing that new wrinkle or added cushion around certain areas of one's anatomy. We can know they exist, but to see them in full view is a little distressing. We suspect for many the health club scene with all its mirrors is a little intimidating. As a result, we tend to avoid mirrors and decorate our bodies to cover those blatant weaknesses.

As we have noted, the human state hates to acknowledge reality. We will do almost anything to avoid and deny it. Don't we normally buy clothes that enhance our physiques? If you have an extra inch or two around your waistline, you don't normally wear tight shirts to show off the soft cushion that hangs over the belt, do you? It's not necessarily vogue for one who is struggling with weight around the thighs and hips to wear a pair of spandex pants in public without having a long T-shirt on that hangs down to the knees. We tend to cover up the areas we think are ugly, areas that may bring us shame or embarrassment. Consider the following illustration. Two guys are going to the beach, one who is muscled and tan and another who possesses a stomach resembling a globe. If the muscled one sheds his shirt will the other be tremendously comfortable and feel he needs to do the same? Or, do you think he will find reasons to keep his shirt on?

Intrinsic with human nature is the need to present a facade, our so-called good side. This can be best illustrated in the beginning of a relationship between a man and a woman. Both dress well and act with the other's best interests in mind at all times. Have you ever noticed how careful you are when you meet someone for the first time? Social graces are politely over-extended and personal strangeness of any sort is carefully masked, at least so we think. How tragic that the best stuff that is displayed in the early stages of the dating game is often nothing more than fear disguised and insecurity seeking affirmation. What a tragedy for the couple who have very little to offer in the months and years to come. They've already played their best hand, and now hold only the less dynamic material which includes the real essence of the individual. Is this why so many relationships do not last as individuals secure the relationship with a self that is fabricated, what they believe the other wants them to be; only to find the true nature of the individual is nothing close to the fabrication?

To illustrate, Mike remembers a time when he was in college and was invited to attend a get together with a few friends. They were invited to have dinner with some girls. Since Mike is Korean-American, his friends decided that Mike would act as if he did not speak English and let them translate for him the entire evening. Now, Mike does not speak any Korean, Chinese, or Japanese, nor do his friends. But with great skill and precision, they rattled off syllables that were first rate and down-right convincing, dialoguing in believable, pretend Japanese. As the evening progressed, Mike was even beginning to understand his friends' translations. It was difficult to maintain the facade the entire evening, but they managed without breaking out in laughter. Finally, as they were getting ready to leave and all standing at the door, the girls told Mike's friends to tell him good-bye and that it was nice to have had him over for dinner. Mike's two partners in crime passed on the bit of information in sophisticated oriental gibberish. Mike then turned to the girls and replied in good-old standard English: "It was nice to have met you and thanks for everything." You should have seen the look on their faces. Mike wasn't sure if they were going into cardiac arrest or if they were going to beat him with chop sticks, but he survived the night.

The point we wish to make here is we show people what we want them to see and often with great success and benefit. Normally, what we don't want them to see is the negative side or bad parts of our lives, usually the persons we really are. To present the real self is difficult and frightening and generally avoided with full passion by the average human being. What complicates the issue even more is that most are not quite sure what the real self is, since our society forces us to compartmentalize our existence. The answer to the question is more accurately explicated by the interrogative, "when." We are most able to define the self when given an atmosphere or setting to do so. A consistent fabric of identity does not make itself present in such a life where various roles or identities are juggled in accordance with the demand or social requirement(s) of the moment. Our identity is then something to be found "out there," not a state we experience within; providing that one believes that perfect union with the self can be had without any external stimuli. The natural status of the human soul is that it defines itself, in part, sometimes in full, in accordance with its surroundings.

A restless sense of being found out or exposed lingers in the heart of everyone. For many, the fear of rejection is a constant. Masking our fear has become quite an art in our society, so much so that we even convince ourselves we aren't afraid. All along, we are ever so careful to avoid the mirror of life which tells us differently.

Many who wrestle with a poor or distorted sense of self hate to see pictures of themselves or view themselves on video. This is all the more true if the person feels less than attractive and overweight. The paradox lies in the tension arising because we really do want to view the self in the portrait, but find tremendous discouragement in what is actually portrayed. To look at the photograph or view the video is painful because of what we see. Unfortunately, reality is never quite what we expect.

It's hard for us to accept what we are. We are too short, too fat, too tall, too dark, or too light. Should we go on? If I can successfully cover up my areas of weakness and imperfection, others will view me in a more positive light.

If you have ever been in a health spa or a body building gym, you found a disconcerting number of mirrors and people who thoroughly enjoy viewing themselves in them. Developing the perfect physique, being healthy, and looking young have always been major parts of our civilized culture. The unwelcome enemy of aging and ultimately death is placated by the exercise and health craze. The quest for the fountain of youth still exists. The drive to be the ultimate in health and appearance is often nothing more than an individual seeking definition from their appearance or better yet, image.

Many define their existence by the mirror of life. People who live according to the mirror thrive off image: For these, looking good, acting properly, being a somebody, and even being with people of significance, is everything. They want you to view their image in the mirror of life, because their image needs you to give life to it.

Many who enter into body building do so to deal with a poor sense of self. For example, a male may feel small in stature and will seek to compensate by adding muscle to his frame. The old classic, *The Wizard of Oz*, is a perfect example of hiding behind an image. The Wizard is nothing but a small, white-haired old man who hides behind a curtain while portraying a frightening image to all who come. Muscles are added to a small and fragile ego to give the illusion that what you see is the man himself, while all along a frightened little boy runs the controls hoping you never look behind the curtain.

The phenomenon might be better explained as illusion. Life is understood to be a screen where images are projected and viewed by all concerned. Oddly enough, everyone seems to know the images are nothing more than wishful creations of the insecure self; nonetheless an agreement to live according to the world of fabricated personhood is enjoyed. Although the emperor is naked, and all know it, the populace is to sit quietly and pretend such is not the case.

Individuals are then free to project whatever they can get away with on the screen. The one who is best able to operate the controls from behind the curtain comes out ahead in the creative game of illusion. As a result, we spend less and less time on the nature of life and more on the illusions we are seeking to maintain. Concern is centered on what is on the screen and not on what is behind the curtain. Personhood becomes fused with image, and only a faint memory of the person behind the curtain remains.

No wonder we are such an anxious people. If anxiety is really nothing more than the fear of life seeking security, we can understand why a person, who is living behind an image, would be nervous of exposure. When there is something to hide, peace is not a mainstay. Only those who have done something wrong find it unnerving when a police officer is around. The presence of the police is not a problem for those who have not broken the law. As a matter of fact, having a police officer around can even be comforting.

The emptiness of the inner life is masterfully hidden behind various images of success, strength, beauty, happiness, and togetherness. Like a china doll, the exterior is quite beautiful and definitely pleasing to the eye. With such beauty, no one cares whether the object is hollow or not. The key to enjoying a china doll is found in our eyes; one enjoys looking at the doll but does not handle it for fear of damage. People who live the shallow existence of the china doll will find they must be handled with care or damage will result.

Since the china doll is meant to be seen only, those who find themselves in this syndrome need their images admired. Without the admiration, life cannot be had for such a person.

Closeness is a frightening and uncomfortable experience for the china doll, for if the image is shattered the result is devastating. All that exists is the image. A fear of nothingness or smallness permeates the hollow world of the person who wrestles with the China Doll Syndrome.

In the world of the china doll, mirrors are everything. They help keep the image sharp and a sense of self evident. If the china doll turns inward she is instantly confronted with the painful experience of emptiness. A sense of self is not present unless the image is visible to the self and to others. As the infant looks to the mother for a sense of safety and well-being, the china doll must look to the mirror image for its sense of security and well-being. Whatever the image might be, it is pampered and handled with extreme care.

Marriage: Mike's Image Killer (Shared in the first person by Mike)

Marriage was the image killer for me. My wife never enjoyed the powerful, together image I portrayed. She always managed to find the curtain and me hiding behind it. She would then proceed to talk to the little guy operating the controls to the image. I would pull the curtain shut and continue to speak to her from my image. As you can, see this would create a rather tense situation. This might surprise you, coming from a pastor, but we would argue from time to time. I would prefer to call them "constructive discussions."

I loved my wife (and still do), yet I found it hard to express that to her face to face. Oh, I had no problem saying "I love you," but looking into her eyes for long, lingering moments and telling her how special she is to me was a definite stretch of my person. A few years back I remember hearing a song that perfectly described how I felt about her. I welled up with emotion as I listened and decided I had to buy the tape and play it for her.

I planned a romantic evening for the two of us and had the tape in the car. On our way to dinner, I put the tape in the cassette deck and told her the song really described my feelings for her. She was intensely interested and hung on every word of the song. I looked down while the song was playing, occasionally glancing over to see her response. When her soft eyes and bright smile met my quick glance, I found myself overcome by embarrassment. How strange to be embarrassed after being married for several years. After the song was finished, I expected her to leap across the seat and hug me. Rather, I looked at her smiling face only to be confronted with a question: "So, what are you trying to say?"

I replied, "Didn't you hear the words?"
"Yes," she said with a smile on her face.

Feeling slightly vulnerable, I offered to play the song for her again. I knew exactly what she wanted. She had pulled the curtain back and asked the little guy behind it how he felt. Of course, the little guy pulled the curtain shut and quickly deferred to the tape for another hearing.

I have had major breakthroughs in my life with my battle with insecurity. As a result, I thought I was pretty much over it until I embarked on my second church plant. As I assumed the pastorate of an empty building, my insecurity was ever increasing. This was regardless of the fact that I had two previously successful ministries, completed my Masters Degree, and had fourteen years of ministry experience under my belt, not to mention the Lord was with me. One would figure I would not feel the sting of insecurity, at least not in the magnitude it presented itself. Facing the challenges of a new ministry, starting from scratch, and leaving those we had come to love were all more difficult than I anticipated.

I found myself tempted to forsake the vision God had planted in my heart, and lured by the enemy to appease the gods of success in our church world. Programs and gimmicks began to run through my mind as ways to bring people to the church while love for the lost gave way to seeking approval from others. I wrestled to fight the temptation to bring an old image back to life--pretending to be someone else was an easy thing for me.

Impressing people and having them stand in awe of my work was always a way for me to find a sense of identity and security, and the enemy knew it. Satan offered the tasty morsel over and over and its aroma was ever so appealing.

Maybe success is less in a formula than in the reality of insecurity. To be free from insecurity, one must come face to face with it. The state of fallen humanity is to try to fix the problem without accepting responsibility for it and/or avoid exposing the problem if at all possible. Like Adam in the garden, we tend to place the blame elsewhere and hide ourselves from the Most High.

The paradox I have found is that the more I am able to admit I am insecure, the less I feel so. The irony is I end up spending less time on pretending to be secure and more on being the man God called me to be. It is when I feel most inadequate that the grace of the Cross is most profound.

I learned this lesson (and am still learning) in a counseling session with a man who had a deep struggle with his identity and depression (I felt like I was counseling myself). He was one of those keen individuals who were bright and quite capable of reading your own struggles. In one of our sessions, he said to me, "I've noticed you struggle with insecurity." In the context of our counseling, the man was not trying to help me but seeking to demonstrate his superiority over me by discrediting me. That would allow him to remove himself from any further need to counsel with me or anyone else. What I realized at that moment was I was trapped. If I denied I was insecure, then he would see through me and probably discontinue counseling. On the other hand, if I admitted I was insecure, then I would have to be insecure. I pondered for a moment and prayed intensely for a few seconds. I responded to the individual's psychological assessment by saying: "You are right. I am insecure. What I have learned is how to take my insecurity to the Father and allow Him to establish me." As I finished saying the statement I felt a sense of freedom and confidence come over me. Paradoxically, I found a deep sense of security in the midst of acknowledging my insecurity.

As the late Dr. William Lane (Former Dean of Religion at Seattle Pacific University) told me in a private conversation, "Our lives are like the velvet cloths used to set jewelry on when displaying them before the customer. The darkness of the cloth reveals, in stark contrast, the brilliance of the diamond. We are the cloths and the cross is the diamond. Our lives are meant to reveal the dynamic nature of the love and mercy of our Lord as was demonstrated at Calvary. Maybe this is what Paul meant when he said, "Therefore I will boast all the more gladly about my weaknesses, so that Christ's power may rest on me" (2 Corinthians 12:9 NIV).

Health Issues: Tom's Image Killer (Shared in first person by Tom)

Growing up as a kid, I was very athletic. This was, in part, due to my Dad, who was a sports nut. He was All-American in basketball in his senior year of high school, and played minor league baseball right after World War II. He was an expert hunter and trout fisherman, and loved to camp. So as the firstborn son, dad did with me what a lot of dads do with their sons - he tried to live vicariously through me. To some extent, this initially lead to great benefit for me - I too became a sportsman, started fishing with him when four years old, and hunting at five. I started junior league baseball and football very early and excelled at both. Over the years I became an expert marksman, taking home lots of game and could fish a trout out of a mountain stream no wider than the length of my pole. To my dad's frustration, basketball was definitely not my thing - I just didn't like it as much as the other sports I was involved in - so I gave up on that early on.

Even as I progressed in my sporting skills, an interesting thing began to happen. Over time, throughout adolescence and my teen years, I became less able to maintain my physical performance level. Doctors told me it was due to Asthma, allergies and a really bad set of sinuses. I couldn't get enough air in and out of my lungs to run, indeed even to walk long distances. By the time I was 21 and in my senior year of college, my lung function prevented me from running the mile in a Physical Education class in the allotted time, causing me to fail the class. The guy my dad had built me to be, the robust, active sportsman, was no longer functioning. Running sports were out, and tromping through the woods in search of game was less and less possible.

Like any young guy, a whole lot of my self-image was built around emulating my father (in this case, a sportsman), and trying to be what he wanted me to be. When I couldn't do that, it left him disappointed and me frustrated. No longer could I do the things I loved to do, and the things I had built my image on, being tall, strong, and athletic, the middle line backer, the centerfielder, the huntsman.

My compensation for this loss of image was to pursue other things and to do so with arrogance. I projected my confidence from the playing field into other areas. I started on a quest to prove myself to the world, and my dad.

Unfortunately, my dad did not live long enough to see any such proof. He died at age 63, when I was just 29. (My mother died one year later, at age 60.) It was not until age 33 that I was diagnosed with Cystic Fibrosis. Now my health history became clear, and the reasons for my declining lung capacity and the resultant effect on my sporting performance made sense. But that didn't clarify my identity issues. It only made them worse. I felt that I was not only an incapable guy, but now I was one with a "terminal" disease. (Most people with CF don't live past age 25-30.) At this time I was in the process of starting my first church and this really took the wind out of my sails. My arrogance was broken down by my limitations in life. The real me was exposed.

The years since my diagnosis have been an era during which I have begun to realize what is important in life from God's perspective. Who I am as a person is far more important to Him than what I do in life, whether it is in sports activities, intellectual pursuits, or in His service. Who I am as a son is what is important to my Father, not what I do as a son. He knows, as I do now also, that if He can perfect my being, He will influence my doing. All we do, in life and ministry, flows from who we are. And in that doing I have come to rely not on my ability, but on the grace empowerment that rests on my life: I am what I am by the grace of God (1 Corinthians 15:10). His grace works powerfully in me and through me, and it is His grace that defines my role in His Kingdom economy and gives me proper self awareness (Romans 12:3-5). Most of all, it is His grace that manifests His love for me and to me as a son. No longer do I need to win acceptance through my efforts - I have it in Him. It is not about my effort or my abilities, but what He has already accomplished in Christ. My arrogance about myself is turning into my confidence in Christ. Who am I? Now I know; I am a portrait of His grace.

Dietrich Bonhoeffer wrote a poem in his prison confinement that graphically depicts the struggle for identity and how one man came to understand it. The last two stanzas of the poem wonderfully illustrate the security that can be found in the insecurity of life.

> Who am I? This or the other?
> Am I one person today, and tomorrow another?
> Am I both at once? A hypocrite before others,
> and before myself a contemptibly woebegone weakling?
> Or is something within me still like a beaten army,
> fleeing in disorder from victory already achieved?
> "Who am I? They mock me, these lonely questions of mine.
> Whoever I am, thou knowest, O God, I am thine. (*Letters and Papers from Prison* 348)

To say I am victorious and riding high on the glory of the Most High would not paint the complete picture. Although I do sense victory in my battle with insecurity, the landscape of my life at present is not as beautiful as I would like to show. As a matter of fact, I still feel insecure at times. Yes, even as I write this.

Life is not about demonstrating how healed I am or about pleasing others or even trying to make a name for myself. It is living for the glory of our God. There is a strange sense of security that comes over me every time I ponder the reality of God being pleased with me in Christ. After all, it is presenting His name to the world that matters. The apostle Paul states it so well. He writes: "But we have this treasure in jars of clay, to show that the surpassing power belongs to God and not to us" (2 Corinthians 4:7). We are nothing more than cracked pots of clay. A word to the wise: Spend less time trying to patch up your cracks and work on letting the brilliance of the treasure shine through each one. Life is not about how good we look or how good we are. It is about how wonderful and merciful our God is as was so powerfully demonstrated at Calvary.

To all the cracked-pots in Christ: Use your insecurity as a weapon.

The Need to Cover up

The problem since the original sin of Adam and Eve is that we are not all that eager for people to see us as we are. We tend to live behind our facades or masks, revealing what we believe people want to see. We spend our lives hiding who we really are, stuffing our secrets under our beds, organizing our chaos into nice and orderly piles, and then dressing them up in ornate ways, all to avoid the exposure of being discovered for who we really are. And yet, our soul longs to be discovered, to be known.

The Bible begins with a beautiful picture of relationship as Adam and Eve enjoy their relationship with God, each other, and creation. There is perfect harmony, absolute trust, and no shame. They were not afraid to be vulnerable, to be themselves fully; after all, they had nothing to hide. There was perfect peace and security for Adam and Eve. Donald Miller, in his excellent book, *Searching For God Knows What*, makes this practical for us as he writes:

> Here is what I think Moses was saying: Man is wired so he gets his glory (his security, his understanding of value, his feeling of purpose, his feeling rightness with his Maker, his security for eternity) from God, and this relationship is so strong, and God's love is so pure, that

Adam and Eve felt no insecurity at all, so much so that they walked around naked and didn't even realize they were naked. (70-71)

All of this security and peace ended the moment Adam and Eve disobeyed God and sinned. Their action disrupted the relationship with God and opened their eyes to a lesser reality that would now dictate and imprison humanity. The shackles of fear and shame became the binding and dominant realities restricting the hearts of Adam and Eve and ours as well.

Let's look at the ancient account of Genesis to see what happened to Adam and Eve after they disobeyed God and ate of the tree of good and evil in Genesis 3:1-13.

In Genesis 3:7, after they disobeyed and ate the fruit, they realized they were naked and sowed fig leaves for covering. The first reaction is to cover up.

Genesis 3:8-10 shows that no longer is intimate fellowship with God possible, now they are afraid and hide. Fear is a predominant feature of the fallen or lesser state. By "lesser" we mean that this existence is not the full and free existence originally designed by God (philosophically called the "penultimate", a contingent existence based upon the "Ultimate" existence). We speak to God behind the bush. More simply, we speak to God behind our coverings. We do not want Him to see us as we really are. Our shame is carefully hidden and is what drives our need to cover and hide. We cannot bear the thought that we stand unclothed before our Maker and that our Maker sees us as we are. As a result, we seek to cover ourselves before God.

In Genesis 3:12, the man cannot take responsibility but blames the woman and ultimately, blames God. We now live lives wherein we find it difficult to take full responsibility.

Adam and Eve find their lives radically changed. They no longer feel safe and find true communion with God and each other nearly impossible. In Genesis we are able to find a rather honest description of human existence. Please note that we are not offering a psychological assessment for various personality disorders but simply suggesting that all human beings are born in this state that Genesis describes after the sin of Adam and Eve. We do understand that life also adds to the dilemma by way of abuse, pain, abandonment, neglect, etc., but this is beyond the scope of our book. Here is what we see in their story:

Realization of nakedness, resulting in shame. We now live our lives based in shame which fears exposure of the self, the loss of control, and vulnerability. No wonder trust and faith become so difficult; it is a relational dynamic that asks for the heart and the trust of another.

Sewing of fig leaves: the covering. We now live our lives behind facades, masks, and the like. Fear and shame dictate such actions, keeping people at arm's length from really knowing who we are.

The hiding behind the bush. We speak to God behind our coverings. Not only do we hide with other human beings, we now hide in our dialogue with God for fear that He might be angry with us for our inappropriate behaviors. We are afraid to simply come from behind the bush and dialogue with our Father in heaven, rather we speak to Him behind our good works hoping that He will find us acceptable and bless us accordingly. We fear being vulnerable or, as Jesus said, "poor in spirit" (Matthew 5:3).

The denial of responsibility. As fallen creatures, living the lesser reality, we have difficulty with responsibility. We either take all the blame or take none, blaming others. Have you ever found it difficult to simply say, "yes, it was my fault" without adding an explanation to it? We are not saying it is wrong to explain, but that it is intensely difficult to accept responsibility without justifying yourself, lightening the responsibility somehow. No one faults the logic of Sarai for engaging in a Plan B which allowed Abram to hurry up the promise of God by having their child of promise with Hagar during their in between season. After all, what would you do when you are pressured to be a mother, waiting on God who hasn't come through, and the daunting reality that you are barren? Or King David saying after sleeping with another man's wife (Bathsheba), "You know, I've been under a lot of pressure lately running the Kingdom" tired, stressed, and feeling alone. Just a momentary lapse of judgment.

The Practical Consequences Explained

As noted earlier, the prophet Jeremiah paints two crucial realities about human existence. The first is we are thirsty people: "My people have committed two sins: They have forsaken me, the spring of living water." The second is we look to find satisfaction for ourselves without God: "and have dug their own cisterns, broken cisterns that cannot hold water" (Jeremiah 2:13 NIV). Since the sin of Adam and Eve we have lived lives that are far less than what God originally designed. We'd like to take a few moments to describe for you practically the results of our fallen state, and the consequences of the sin of our First Parents:

The first consequence is a broken relationship with God. Prior to the Fall (Adam and Eve's sin which disrupted their relationship with God) the woman and man were in perfect relationship with God. Man, who was in perfect communion with God, is now described in terms of fear, hiding, and fleeing before God. Relationship with God has now changed to involve elements that were previously not present. The sin act created a barrier between the first couple and God. An antidote was needed for the relationship to be restored. The relationship of peace and harmony changed to displeasure and disharmony. The curse sanctions bring difficulty and disharmony to life. No longer will humanity find dominion over the earth as something cooperating with his efforts. A bit of good news in this is discovered as we see in the curse sanctions: It is imperative to note the serpent is the only one cursed. Adam and Eve are not cursed as persons.

The second consequence is that shame and fear is now a normal part of everyday life as we see the first pair move into a life of hiding from the Most High. Anxiety is now a common emotion in life.

The first couple now fears being exposed and seeks to avoid it. "Once they chose to be other than what they were, they became naked and ashamed" (Bradshaw viii). Shame causes individuals to keep a part of themselves from others. Practically speaking, shame causes you to keep the person you really feel yourself to be hidden. Shame can have both good and bad aspects to it.

On the good side, healthy shame is that which helps us realize we are not God, helps us accept our humanness. In this sense, it gives us permission to be human. However, people have a difficult time understanding the difference between being bad at something and being bad overall. Healthy shame then gives us boundaries and limits. Without these we would be confused and waste enormous amounts of emotional and physical energy. Shame is the emotional energy that tells us that we are not God; that we are human and will make mistakes. In simple language, shame tells us that we need help. We need Christ.

On the negative side, unhealthy shame can move us to believe we are bad in and of ourselves. With this, unhealthy shame moves us to believe we are mistakes. This can lead to "soul murder" (Alice Miller's term), a killing of the self. If we are ashamed of whom we are, then we will do whatever we can to hide who we are. People will then act in ways that elevate themselves (the arrogant or over confident person) or to destroy the self (the individual who beats himself up or is always down on himself).

Elevate the self-------------------------Destroy the self

What lies at the heart of unhealthy shame is the fear of exposure. Shame is ultimately internalized when one is abandoned. The final result of toxic shame is that of alienation and isolation which leads to the creation of the false self. Worth becomes something measured on the outside, by performance or looks, and not by what is on the inside. Saul illustrates for us a life of shame that uses the language of smallness to describe itself. Throughout the king's life, he wrestled with insecurity, giving way to raging jealousy and envy over the life of a young shepherd boy named, David.

> Just then Saul approached Samuel at the gateway and asked, "Can you please tell me where the seer's house is?"
>
> "I am the seer!" Samuel replied. "Go on up the hill ahead of me to the place of sacrifice, and we'll eat there together. In the morning I will tell you what you want to know and send you on your way. And don't worry about those donkeys that were lost three days ago, for they have been found. And I am here to tell you that you and your family are the focus of all Israel's hopes."
>
> Saul replied, *"But I'm only from Benjamin, the smallest tribe in Israel, and my family is the least important of all the families of that tribe! Why are you talking like this to me?"*(1 Samuel 9:18-21 NLT)

Saul believed he was of little or no consequence, basing his reality upon his understanding of himself which was for him the seedbed of fear. Fear has been described as that feeling of not being at home, of feeling uncanny and lost in the universe. Due to this separation from God, each individual realizes there is something not right within them. Brunner describes this fear as "difficulty of breathing - angustiae - the suffocating distress which the soul feels in its separation from God" (195). Have you noticed how you pant lately?

In spite of this, God seeks to restore the creation to Himself. This is evidenced in Genesis 3:15, the "Proto euangelion" (the first gospel). The word "seed" is singular, which is a reference to Christ. In other words, in the midst of the curse sanctions, God provides a note of hope for the human race. God also makes a garment of skin for Adam and Eve, not because their garments were lacking, but to set the stage for the Divine mercy, which seeks to cover the sin of all with His freeing love.

The third consequence is internal conflict. Human nature is not at rest. We are not at home with ourselves. Augustine tells us "our hearts find no peace until they rest in you" (21).

As a result, we are a bored society. Complicating this reality has been the technological advances in the past 50 years. With the ability to relieve pain and make life more simplified, we have found the opposite to be the case: increased pain and lives that are more complicated. Pascal used the term "ennui," meaning being bored, which can be another way of saying life is empty.

As we noted for you earlier, this emptiness or internal boredom is manifest quite acutely in the phrase, "to kill time." Too often the phrase is articulated by people who are completely unaware of the tension they feel in life. Let me explain that time is a basic component of life, a substratum of human existence. It is, essentially, a fundamental element to human existence, the very element we are wishing to kill. Brunner adds:

> Existence in time cannot be endured; people flee from it into a sham existence, into a life where they can forget themselves. Not only the greater part of our obvious pleasure, sport and play, but also a good deal of our highly intellectual pursuit of culture, is at bottom nothing more or less than a 'pastime' of this kind, by means of which--although it is impossible to satisfy the empty soul--it is at least possible to fill it; it is a narcotic with which the hunger of the soul is to some extent doped. (*Man in Revolt* 196)

The fourth consequence is external conflict. In the beginning, there was environmental and relational harmony. After the Fall, we have conflict in both arenas. The man and the woman find the results of their disobedience as follows: To the woman, pain in childbearing and to be ruled by her husband. To the man, painful toil in an environment that will not cooperate now. To both, death. "Just as man is destined to die once, and after that to face judgment" (Hebrews 9:27 NIV).

Thus far we have learned that human beings live in fear and hiding, unable to take full responsibility for their lives, adding to the difficulty of trusting God, especially when we are in the in between.

We also indicated that life is not always about what took place (the event), but about how we interpreted what happened to us. Again, this is not to say that it doesn't matter what happens to us, but to assert that we have the ability to perceive and interpret events. Our emotions then are a product of how we have perceived the event, not the event itself (e.g. S=situation, I=interpretation, R=response). We are not the sum total of our past experiences. Again, all of this makes it even more difficult to interpret correctly what God is doing when the promise is delayed. If our parents neglected us, abandoned us, or we have had our trust violated, then trusting God when the promise seems like it's not going to come to pass is rather difficult. Trusting God in the in between of life is like walking right into our worst fear or nightmare. That is, we are people who have interpreted their past in a certain light, forming a worldview that includes the following:

S = Situation: Life that is happening in the present moment.

I = Interpretation: Our interpretation of what is happening in the present moment based on our relational and circumstantial worldview.

This includes our *relational worldview* - how I view myself, how I view others and how I view God; and our *circumstantial worldview* - how I view the past, how I view the present and how I view the future.

R= *Response:* What I will do now, based on my worldview in this moment of in between. Our response may or may not interpret reality correctly. If we do not interpret correctly, the pain of our past continues. Even if we do interpret correctly we are more apt to be able to respond to what is because we are not living in the past, trying to fix it, or living in the future by trying to protect it - that is from becoming our past or our fear.

Emotions: Our "Check Engine" Light

Dealing with reality is never an easy thing. It is precisely what makes the in between of life so difficult. It is during the in between of life that we are radically confronted with the reality of our lives, exposed for who we really are, and invited to face our fears.

Our automobiles have a nice feature in them that lets us know when something is wrong with the car. Each car has a little orange light that tells us that there is something wrong with the engine. It is a warning light that suggests that we might want to have the car checked out by a mechanic, deal with the problem. There are three responses one can choose from when dealing with their check engine light: we *cover* (suppress) it with tape so one does not notice it. We *smash* (express) out the light with a hammer. Or we *respond* (acknowledge) as the manufacturer intended by looking under the hood or fixing the problem.

In much the same way, our emotions are like the check engine lights in our cars. They tell us that there is something wrong, just as feelings do with our physical bodies. When we feel pain in our physical bodies, like a burning sensation when we touch something, the pain causes us to quickly move our hands away from the object. Pain can then be helpful, but if you don't feel the pain you are in danger of serious injury (e.g. leprosy).

We must keep in mind that our emotions are amoral. They are neither good nor bad. Emotions are simply a part of our humanity. Trying to deal with our emotions is like fighting the air, for there is nothing to grab. What is more important is how we respond to our emotions. We can either deal with them or not. Our responses can include the options of covering, breaking, or acknowledge them.

We can cover the check engine light. Emotionally speaking, what we often do is simply suppress it. Suppression, simply defined, is a conscious denial of feelings, whereas repression is an unconscious denial. Open up to God while you still can, because bottling up your feelings too long will disrupt your relationship with Him. Like floodwaters, our emotions will build up and we will find it incredibly difficult to turn to God. If nothing else, it disrupts the harmony of our relationship with Him. King David says it well.

> When I refused to confess my sin,
> I was weak and miserable,
> and I groaned all day long.
> Day and night your hand of discipline was heavy on me.
> My strength evaporated like water in the summer heat.
> Finally, I confessed all my sins to you
> and stopped trying to hide them.
> I said to myself, "I will confess my rebellion to the LORD."
> And you forgave me! All my guilt is gone.
> Therefore, let all the godly confess their rebellion to you while there is time, that they may not drown in the floodwaters of judgment.
> (Psalm 32:3-6 NLT)

We can break the check engine light. Emotionally speaking, what we are dealing with here is full expression: This is nothing more than blowing off steam and letting people know how you feel, being the honest person that says what they think all the time without considering how others feel. Expression may help one to feel better but often at the expense of others. "There I'm glad I got that off my chest," you may say after an outburst. But in the process you have destroyed your husband, wife or children. James warns us, "My dear brothers and sisters, be quick to listen, slow to speak, and slow to get angry. Your anger can never make things right in God's sight" (James 1:19-20 NLT).

Or we can respond to the check engine light by acknowledging our emotions and trying to understand what they are telling us. This is the most important aspect to being transformed. If we can become honest and admit to the issues or emotions we are feeling, then we will be better equipped to understand what is going on within and surrender that aspect of our lives to the Lord and trust Him fully in the in between.

Often, in Christianity, we hide how we truly feel because we believe it is not right for a Christian to have anger. The Bible is full of angry responses from godly people (Psalm 109:1-13). It is always alright for us to dump our pain, hurt, and anger to the Lord. As we do, it keeps us from dumping it on someone else.

Masks: Covering the "Check Engine" Light

Since human nature hides, it is apparent that people have a tendency to not really show who they are and this is particularly true during our seasons of in between. In other words, people wear masks to cover their true identity, their pain, fears, etc.

The practical reason we wear masks is that somewhere along life's journey our hearts were deeply wounded, abandoned, forgotten, neglected, passed over, or the like. When Mike was a young boy it was clear to him that his dad wanted him to have round eyes like he did, not the slanted (Asian), squinty ones that he had. Mike also understood that his mom wanted him to obey at all costs, although, had she known, the issue of obedience to dad would not have been a problem. The mask Mike learned to utilize from this painful situation was one of performance, hiding the disappointment of his heart because he believed no one really wanted to know him as he was, and always appearing sweet, happy, and strong. After all, it was only the good-looking, all-together kid his dad wanted in the first place.

The wound that Mike experienced was one of rejection for who he was because "I'm not good enough as I am." The way Mike chose to compensate for this was to put on the performance or Princess Fiona mask. If there is ever a season that tempts us into wearing our masks or putting them back on, it is the season of in between. Tom's experience was similar, as he was also seeking his father's approval, only to have his mask (he chose the Data/Spock version) ripped away by his physical frailty.

Simply put, we wear masks for many reasons. We are afraid, so we hide our true identity. We believe people will not like what they see without the mask. We believe that the mask is what people want. Our society helps facilitate this through the worship of wealth, beauty, etc. There is a powerful episode in the old series *The Twilight Zone* that depicts the quest for beauty. A woman is badly disfigured and the doctors are trying to repair her. When her face bandages are removed the doctors move away in horror at the ugly sight. The camera takes the viewpoint of the disfigured woman, and you are able to see each bandage removed until she can see clearly. As the bandages come off, the woman's eyes lay hold of the doctors before her, and what she sees are doctors with radically disfigured faces moving away from her in horror. When the camera turns to show us the woman, we find a beautiful woman as we would describe beauty. However, in this world, beauty is not the same. And so, what is deemed beautiful by our society is considered horrific in this one.

Another reason for masks is so that we can control pain better. That is, when people reject us or hurt us, we know they are not really rejecting or hurting who we really are. It is safer to keep a distance. The mask operates like a fight with the self. It is safer to knock yourself out then let another do it. As silly as this sounds you are familiar with the pain of knocking yourself out and you know you won't annihilate yourself. If you allow another that opportunity, you don't know what they will do. It is this fear of the unknown that helps us keep our masks on.

Over all, the mask helps us feel better about ourselves. We feel like we can do more and be more behind the mask. With that said, let us list for you some masks we might be hiding behind. Keep in mind this is not an exhaustive list.

The Data Mask: This is the mask of intelligence and rationality - no or little emotion is permitted (e.g. Mr. Spock or Mr. Data of Star Trek).

The Shrek Mask: Like the character Shrek, this person acts big to protect the small fragile ego - acts like they are always doing fine and needing nothing.

The Princess Fiona Mask: This is the person who hides behind their looks, success, money, etc., and keeps people at arm's length because they fear if people get too close they'll discover that she is really an ogre. Self-contempt is strong here in anticipation of rejection, and there is a rejection of self before others reject it.

The Friendly Nark Mask: This person never assumes responsibility and spends most of their time judging and criticizing others. Although this person might be critical or blame others for their issues, the problem is one of not taking responsibility more than being critical.

The Eeyore Mask: "Why bother," as Eeyore would say. It won't work out anyway. This individual believes that, no matter what happens, it will always be negative.

The Porcupine Mask: This individual has various relational styles that keep people at arm's length. The individual is not always aware they are doing this. The lack of trust has allowed for these quills to develop to protect the individual from further harm. This person will find himself or herself alone and will hate it while simultaneously not understanding why people will not come any closer.

The Pharisee Mask: This person is quick to judge others, likes to talk about people and quick to disguise it as a desire to pray for someone, critical of people who are not godly, or really being like them. In reality, this person acts in ways that are contrary to what he really feels or does, the classic hypocrite.

The Incredible Hulk Mask: This individual is impatient, quick-tempered, judgmental, and tends to be demanding.

The Constant Comic Mask: Individual utilizes humor and sarcasm to deal with pain, redirecting anger by way of jokes and/or sarcasm. It is hard to get a serious or real emotional response from this person. On the other hand, an individual might use humor to bring peace to situations, the Placater or Fixer types.

The Martha Mask: This is the person who is afraid to stop, because it is the doing that provides identity and protects the heart, e.g. the workaholic. In churches sometimes this is the one who serves the most but not for the right reasons. Mary was content to sit at Jesus' feet, but Martha had to keep moving.

The Sweet and Syrupy Mask: This person acts in ways that are kind and sweet. In reality, they are full of anger and rage. They are fearful of what is inside or what they do not know, and have discovered kindness as a great means to cope with the pain within.

For now, let us offer the key to living life in between. It is being honest and admitting to the pain and disappointment of life, as well as acknowledging how you protect yourself and surrendering your heart to God's process, surrendering your future, your dreams, your mask, and your light to Him (you do this by blowing out your torch which is the way you control your life. See Isaiah 50:10-11 and read it and answer the question, "what is my torch?" - more on this later).

Say It Isn't So

As we have been suggesting, the real nature of life is far from satisfying. Adding to our dilemma is the innate resistance to acknowledging what is real and our ability to hide behind images and masks, living out the lie of the matrix. Our personal worlds are not what we like them to be, but very few dare to profess such.

The professors of the "see good in everything" mindset are promoting a helpful philosophy. To purposely see hope in bad situations is definitely uplifting for the psyche and healthy for our bodies. However, is simply hoping the cure-all? A more prominent issue involves the object of our hope.

Exactly what are we supposed to hope in? Human goodness? What kind of hope do you give a terminally ill patient?

Maybe seeing the good in every situation is not enough. Acknowledging truth or what is might be the preferred approach. But again, we do not normally like to hear truth, especially if it's painful. As the photograph tells all, pressing behind the image exposes the little man behind the curtain, shouting to the world that the wonderful Wizard of Oz is a small old man.

Rather than deal with the truth, we opt for a sham existence that cannot be sufficiently dealt with without the aid of some narcotic: drugs; alcohol; play; sex; work; church; etc. In the midst of such a world, no wonder we find it is so difficult living in between. There is something about the in between of life that pulls back the curtain and reveals the true nature of who we are and our world, exposing the matrix for what it is, a lie. Can we ever overcome such an obstacle and learn to embrace the promise as we journey in the in between?

SECTION TWO

Life in the Middle

For I consider that the sufferings of this present time are not worth comparing with the glory that is to be revealed to us. For the creation waits with eager longing for the revealing of the sons of God. For the creation was subjected to futility, not willingly, but because of him who subjected it, in hope that the creation itself will be set free from its bondage to decay and obtain the freedom of the glory of the children of God. For we know that the whole creation has been groaning together in the pains of childbirth until now. And not only the creation, but we ourselves, who have the firstfruits of the Spirit, groan inwardly as we wait eagerly for adoption as sons, the redemption of our bodies. For in this hope we were saved. Now hope that is seen is not hope. For who hopes for what he sees? But if we hope for what we do not see, we wait for it with patience. (Romans 8:18-25)

CHAPTER SEVEN

Life as Maintenance: "The Maintenance Agreement"

Complacency - The Killer

In our culture the lure to security and blind acceptance is fast becoming the normal mode of living. The tragedy of our blind acceptance is the ironic reality that we question what is true and accept what is false. Although we are a searching society, we find ourselves searching in arenas where life cannot be found. We are in such a hurry to secure our worlds and find comfort that we are prone to take anyone's word, providing they are somewhat of an expert either by way of training or experience - the latter being more acceptable.

As a result, pressing for the fullness of Kingdom living is not a part of the average Christian's spiritual agenda. "As long as life is comfortable and peaceful, I am ok and don't need to really stretch myself" might be the underlying thought processes of many in the faith.

Growth in Christ can only come by death to ourselves, hope in Him, faith in His character, and self-denial. Dallas Willard had this to say:

> Some time ago I came to realize that I did not love the people next door. They were, by any standards, dangerous and unpleasant people--ex-bikers who made their living selling drugs.
>
> ...I realized how little I truly cared for nearly all the people I deal with through the day, even when on 'religious business.' I had to

admit that I had never earnestly sought to be possessed by God's kind of love, to become more like Jesus. Now it was time to seek.

> ...Living under the governance of heaven frees and empowers us to love as God loves. But outside the safety and sufficiency of heaven's rule, we are too frightened and angry to really love others, or even ourselves, and so we arrange our dreary substitutes...'What's so great if you love those who love you? Terrorists do that! If that's all your love amounts to, God certainly is not involved. Or suppose you are friendly to our kind of people. So is the Mafia! (29-31)

Are we accepting our call and living a life that is full of abundance, or are we comparing ourselves to other Christians, and as a result settling for something less than what God has for us? (See Galatians 6:1-5). Paul instructs us to not compare ourselves with others, but we are to test our own work. We are to answer to God for the things we do and not rate ourselves in accordance with what others do and say.

Living Life in Maintenance Mode

There are only two choices of how you are going to live your life. You will either live it in maintenance mode, or in seeking after God, His presence and purposes for you. God gives each of us promises in life, part of that larger future and hope He has for us in the kingdom yet to come. What Hell would like to do is cut you a deal. That's right; the Devil has got a deal for you! He wants you to sign off on a maintenance agreement in which you settle for less than God's first, best destiny for you, and he will take it easy on you. Now, we know the Enemy is a liar, and only comes to steal and kill and destroy (John 10:10), but each of us will face this temptation in life. Jesus did, in His Wilderness Temptation in Luke 4: There was the temptation to *self-doubt* and *doubt God's promises* (verse 3). The temptation here for Jesus was to doubt His divinity. Then there is the temptation to *comfort yourself* (verse 4). Here not only could Jesus prove Himself, He could give in during His fast and find self-comfort. He overcame this and waited for the angels to minister to him. Next is the temptation to *"settle"* (verses 5-8), and the deal-cutting is now on in earnest. This deal would have been a shortcut, giving Him rulership without having to go to the Cross. It was also a temptation to doubt the Father's promise to Him of eternal rule. The temptation to *prove yourself* (verses 9-12) is an attempt to get Jesus to cross a boundary with the Father by using His power to demonstrate who He was. It was a temptation to justify Himself. He chose to wait to have the One who is just, to do so.

When you receive a promise, watch out for temptation. You will be tempted to doubt God's promises, to doubt yourself as a son or daughter of Him, to not press on in Christ and settle for less, to cut a deal with yourself, with others, and ultimately with the Devil himself and to prove or justify yourself, your words or your actions. Responding wrongly to any or all of these temptations will leave you despairing of any hope of receiving the promise. It will negate your ability to engage God around the promise He has given you, and cloud your vision and frustrate your faith.

You need to tell the Enemy, and yourself, "no deal!" Settling for a more comfortable existence has already been discussed, and is at the core of all these temptations. There is a purpose in God's Kingdom for you, and you must press on until you have it, whether it lies in this life or the next.

> But whatever gain I had, I counted as loss for the sake of Christ. Indeed, I count everything as loss because of the surpassing worth of knowing Christ Jesus my Lord. For his sake I have suffered the loss of all things and count them as rubbish, in order that I may gain Christ and be found in him, not having a righteousness of my own that comes from the law, but that which comes through faith in Christ, the righteousness from God that depends on faith-- that I may know him and the power of his resurrection, and may share his sufferings, becoming like him in his death, that by any means possible I may attain the resurrection from the dead.
>
> Not that I have already obtained this or am already perfect, but I press on to make it my own, because Christ Jesus has made me his own. Brothers, I do not consider that I have made it my own. But one thing I do: forgetting what lies behind and straining forward to what lies ahead, I press on toward the goal for the prize of the upward call of God in Christ Jesus. (Philippians 3:7-14)

CHAPTER EIGHT

Life as Tension: "Living in the Middle"

Tuning a guitar is a necessary process if one desires to play the instrument with any success or pleasure. There is nothing quite like the discordant sound of a guitar that is out of tune. The more out of tune it is the more painful one finds the sound. The steady and often tedious process of tuning a guitar well is not only necessary but vital for expressing the music that is buried within the heart of the musician. As the strings are being tuned a precise tension is a must for that particular string as it exists in relationship to the other five strings. Without proper tension the strings will not be in tune. The guitar strings find their proper tune in the midst of tension; being at just the right tension allows for melodious music to come from the guitar. One wonders if this is applicable to life as well.

Life is like a guitar, full of tension and in need of proper tuning. Maybe we can say that without proper tension, life will not be lived with any great success or melodic beauty. The problem with this metaphor is that humans tend to greatly resist tension. We prefer control, living on either the active side of life, taking control or charge of our lives, the control posture, or we take the passive side, letting others dictate our lives, the victim posture.

A Grammar Lesson: Living in the Middle Voice

Of the grammatical choices of life, the active voice, passive voice, and the middle voice, the middle voice is what is often forsaken as we opt for the more comfortable options of the active or passive modes of existence. The reason we opt for them is that they both allow a sense of control to be engaged. Even if the control is an illusion, we still feel more comfortable being in control of our lives.

Grammatically speaking, in the active voice the subject is the acting agent, the one, or thing, that performs the action. In the passive voice, the subject is the recipient of the action.

There is an obvious tension in life that is not easily resolved. We find ourselves living lives that seek out solutions and control to the dilemma of humanness. In other words, we do all that we possibly can to control the mystery of life. Sadly, once the mystery is destroyed, there is nothing left but empty areas of the soul that need filling. Maybe this is why we are so bored. A predictable life may have a sense of security to it but it is also rather mundane and boring. To solve the dilemma of life we either take control or charge of our lives, which is to live in the active voice. Or we let others dictate our lives, choosing to live in the passive voice, living out the life as a victim.

Both reactions to the complexity of life resolve the immediate tension we feel. After all, how do we find hope and security in a world that makes little sense? There are times that we pray and nothing happens, and times we do not pray and someone is healed. We live in righteousness, doing all we can to honor God and our life falls apart. Others opt to live in self-absorbed bitterness and greed and oddly enough live blessed lives. It is easy to understand why people opt to take control of their lives. Since no one else will watch out for us, we might as well do it. This even explains why people choose the passive role of victim. They can't control anything; they are just pawns in the massive chess game of life, so why bother?

However, there is another option that is not regularly considered. It is the option to live life in the middle voice. The middle voice is a voice that indicates that the subject is the actor and acts upon himself or herself reflexively. Grammar books define the middle voice as "that use of the verb which describes the subjects participating in the results of the action" (Dana & Mantey 157). Dana & Mantey go on to illustrate that the active voice (e.g. "I counsel"), places its emphasis on the action. The middle voice places its emphasis on the agent (e.g. "I take counsel"); the subject acts with a view of participating in the action.

Is this not an excellent description of the Christian life? In order for us to grasp a sense of who we are, we must first come to realize we were built for the middle voice. We do not control the action. We are not the prime subjects in the sentence or story of life. That is God's role. All too often, Christians incorporate the ancient pagan concept of religion as they pray and attempt to move God so that He might act according to their agenda.

This is why life in between is so difficult to comprehend; it eludes our grasp, our ability to control, to trust in principles or steps to secure our blessed state. It thrusts us face to face with God in a personal relational encounter that leaves us in the present trusting God for our daily allotment of bread. Maybe this is all that God is after.

On the other side of the grammatical spectrum we must realize that one is not controlled by the action; that is a Hindu concept of religion that affords us the permission to sit passively by as the gods or fate exercise their will upon humanity. We are not simply the recipients of the action, but are acted upon without any say in the matter. There is an element of responsibility that we must acknowledge and embrace. Like the guitar, we are attempting to tune ourselves to the key of life that has been provided by God, hoping that the tension will result in a melodious song from our lives.

Living life in the middle voice is learning to accept the mystery of life, acknowledging the tension we face in life, and embracing it. It is realizing that God is moving in our world and we have the privilege of participating in the results. We are not the ones who neither control our destinies nor are our destinies controlled completely by another. We must allow the tension to exist, letting it pull us to the right pressure so that our lives will be in tune, living between the polarities of God's sovereign and all powerful, all knowing will and the free will or volitional power of every human being to choose.

In the in between of life, the guitar is tuned between the polarities of God being all-loving, all-powerful and all-knowing, and the freedom of the saint to choose, whether the saint chooses knowledge over obedience, trusting in the self more than God, or chooses to trust God more than the self. We were not created with responsibility as much as we were

> ...created in 'response-ability.' That is, Adam was made to respond to God, as was so powerfully illustrated when his bodily existence was animated by the very breath of God (Genesis 2:7). Adam became a living person, not because he took life by the horns and embraced it, but rather received it. Adam was not a self-made man that was rugged and independent. He was dependent, while having dominion and authority; he recognized clearly his need for God. Rather, Adam and Eve were created to respond to the love and grace of God. It is their response to Him, receiving the life He gave that allowed them to do all that He commanded. It is then when we respond first to Him that we find we have the ability to do all that He asks of us. (Johnston & Perkinson 47-48)

It is the mystery that His will, along with ours, is fully engaged in the process of life. We are participants in the divine drama that has already been told and acted out by millions and yet is still unfolding in our lives. The drama finds its introduction and conclusion in Jesus Christ, as it plays out the themes of life, loss, suffering, joy, victory, death, and ultimate triumph over and over again in the actors of the play. The themes are being played out in our lives, tuning us to the proper tension that allows our lives to play the song we were created to play as the Divine musician works with His living guitar/creation, tuning and playing in us the song of eternity. To somehow explain this to our satisfaction destroys the element of faith and vibrancy of life that is meant to be experienced in the mystery we call life.

Is Your Guitar Tuned to the Right Key?

Jesus articulated what life in the middle voice looks like in the Lord's Prayer: "Give us our food for today" (Matthew 6:11 NLT). It is interesting that Jesus offers such a prayer. The logic of God is rather indescribable at times and this is one of those times. From a human perspective, a pragmatic, sensible approach to life, one would think it would be better to come to God and ask Him for a storehouse of bread, not just enough for the day. After all, God can give us not just enough for the day, but enough for a lifetime. It would be prudent, one would think, that we get this mere physical need taken care of so that we can get on with more weighty matters of justice, love, mercy, and saving lives. Why waste time asking for such menial things when God could simply give it up front and then, we could make better use of our prayer time for others?

It sounds logical and even right because that is how we often handle our business exchanges, doing our best to maximize the time we have so that we might accomplish the mission and objectives of our corporation. It appears in the Lord's Prayer that God is not being as efficient with His time with us as He could or should be. We are sure God is maximizing His time with us in ways we cannot comprehend but one wonders if we have fully understood His mission.

Could God give us a storehouse of bread? Absolutely! Then why doesn't He? Most likely because we would place our trust in the storehouse and not in God: Having a storehouse would cause us to go to the storehouse and not to Him. This is not to imply that God does not want to bless us with abundance. We believe He does. Rather, it is to argue that human nature has a propensity in trusting itself and finding ways, systems, and principles that might allow for storehouses to be constructed alleviating the anxiety of our souls. Or so we think. "Some trust in chariots and some in horses, but we trust in the name of the LORD our God" (Psalm 20:7 NIV). What are your chariots and horses?

Years ago, Mike was told a story of a Christian professor who had just bought a home. He was being rather pensive one day when a friend asked him, "What are you thinking about?" The professor responded, "It is interesting that before I bought this house I was always fearful that I would never have a home of my own. Now that I own this home I am fearful that I might lose it."

On one side of the fence is fear or anxiety that we will not have the life we so desire. On the other side of the fence we find fear or anxiety that we will lose the life we now have. Maybe these are the tension points of the guitar of life that we need God to tune, allowing Him to stretch us to the necessary, proper tension.

We have already stated that balance is a lie. Trying to balance life will only lead to a life of control and undue stress. We must give up our attempts to balance life and find ways we can participate with God in what He is doing in creation and in our lives. We join Him in His Story, finding our purpose for existence, enjoying the benefits of being His son/daughter, and trusting Him with every breath we take. The right key for tuning one's guitar (life) is found in the key of trust (see Hebrews 11:6).

When we find ourselves in the in between it is easy to conclude that Christianity is not easy and that God is not safe. Lucy embodies this for us, in C. S. Lewis' classic, *The Lion, The Witch, and the Wardrobe*, as she asks Mr. Beaver if Aslan, the lion (figure of Christ) is safe. Mr. Beaver responds by saying that the great Aslan is not safe, but he is good (146). If God is good, then it will take trust or faith to place our lives in His hand, especially when the promise seems far off and the danger of life looming. Let God tune you to the key of trust as you sit between the polarities of His goodness and your pain.

CHAPTER NINE

Life as the Appetizer: "Whetting Your Appetite"

One of the many privileges we have in life is that of going out to dinner with family and friends. There is a quiet delight in being able to enjoy an evening together with people we love, feasting on the delights of the creative geniuses in the culinary arena. May God increase their tribe as we so appreciate their talent. As a matter of fact, the artistic creations at some places almost leave one hesitant to destroy their work of art, with emphasis on "almost."

When you go out to eat the server usually asks you if you would like an appetizer, or a sampler dish of all the appetizers, to relish in before your main course arrives. What is tantalizing about an appetizer is that it not only looks and smells good, it is absolutely delicious, mouth watering, deeply fulfilling and not only whets the appetite, it also reminds us that there is something more delightful and delicious on its way. The entrée, the main course, the full deal is still to come. It makes one hungry just thinking about it. The stomach shouts, "Wow, if the appetizer is this good I can't wait for the main course!"

What a perfect picture of life here on planet Earth. Our present and momentary existence here is an appetizer, a sampler plate that whets our appetite for the main entrée yet to come. Maybe this is what the wise sage of Ecclesiastes had in mind when he penned the insightful thought, "He has planted eternity in the human heart, but even so, people cannot see the whole scope of God's work from beginning to end" (Ecclesiastes 3:11 NLT). "Eternity in the human heart" helps us understand this existence in the here and now as the appetizer of something more to come.

On the negative side the soul whispers, "Is this all there is?" No matter how wonderful life is there is that sense that there is supposed to be something else. The "splinter in the mind" irritates our conscious thoughts: Something is wrong in the land of make-believe. Like Neo, we know there is something wrong. We can feel it, taste it, and sense it. It's almost as if we were not really made for this existence.

On a more positive note, like the appetizer, life is good and we are enjoying it and grateful for the benefits we have, loving our Creator, His creatures and His creation. We find joy in the appetizer but find ourselves longing for the main entrée, the main course, the full deal. We look forward with hopeful anticipation to eternity, to heaven, to being with Jesus. The Psalmist says it well: "The one thing I ask of the LORD-the thing I seek most-is to live in the house of the LORD all the days of my life, delighting in the LORD's perfections and meditating in his Temple" (Psalm 27:4). Paul makes this even simpler for us as he writes about the appetizer:

> All creation anticipates the day when it will join God's children in glorious freedom from death and decay. For we know that all creation has been groaning as in the pains of childbirth right up to the present time. And even we Christians, although we have the Holy Spirit within us as a foretaste of future glory, also groan to be released from pain and suffering. We, too, wait anxiously for that day when God will give us our full rights as his children, including the new bodies he has promised us. Now that we are saved, we eagerly look forward to this freedom. For if you already have something, you don't need to hope for it. But if we look forward to something we don't have yet, we must wait patiently and confidently (Romans 8:20-25 NLT).

Eat all the Courses

Knowing that the main entrée is found in our life in the Kingdom not yet here, there could be a temptation to try to skip the appetizer which is this life. Because of the tension we face living in between many Christians try to not engage in this life, focusing rather on the fullness of the meal to come. This is escapism, plain and simple. The difficulties presented by this life, all the relational conflicts, all of the stress acquired from hopes deferred, make us seek to tunnel under our blankets, to hunker down until the Rapture Bus arrives to take us to the marriage supper of the Lamb.

Sorry, folks, but we are here to tell you that through His death and resurrection, Jesus purchased the "full meal deal" for you, and for you to accept anything less than that is to cut one of those deals with the Devil we have already talked about. Jesus came that you might have life, and have it to the full (John 10:10 NLT), now, as well as forever. You must engage in the appetizer of this life, if you expect to attend the banquet in the future Kingdom. Just for your information, there are lots of Jesus' teachings that indicate that we should not offend the Host! So, enjoy the appetizer, and let the anticipation of the future whet your appetite!

We Groan

As we await the main entrée, enjoying the appetizer called life, the apostle Paul offers hope and encouragement as he informs us that the Holy Spirit will be with us: "And the Holy Spirit helps us in our distress. For we don't even know what we should pray for, nor how we should pray. But the Holy Spirit prays for us with groanings that cannot be expressed in words" (Romans 8:26 NLT).

To the congregation in Corinth Paul wrote these words describing a life of anticipation as we await our main entrée: "Meanwhile we groan, longing to be clothed with our heavenly dwelling" (2 Corinthians 5:2 NIV). "Sighing" or "groaning" is what characterizes our mortal existence. At best, this life is not what we were built for. The apostle goes on to say: "For while we are in this tent, we groan and are burdened, because we do not wish to be unclothed but to be clothed with our heavenly dwelling, so that what is mortal may be swallowed up by life" (2 Corinthians 5:4 NIV).

Paul's use of "stenazomen" ("to groan" occurs here in Romans 5:4 and Romans 8:23) suggests that it is in anticipation of something to come that one groans, not in distress over what is. The idea of groaning here is more in line groaning with eager anticipation for the main course or what is yet to come. It is like the sprinter finishing the race with a groan as he strains forward at the finish line, not out of desperation but in anticipation of the victory. As wonderful as the appetizer might be, it is not fulfilling and only takes the edge of the hunger, reminding us there is more. Our passion for that something more is still there. Ralph Martin makes a rather helpful comment:

> The groaning is in conjunction with the help of the Spirit, itself a gift of God, for we groan eagerly (Rom. 8:25; cf. 5:5.). Why groan eagerly with the Holy Spirit's indwelling unless there was something

good to follow? The groaning in Rom. 8:23 is a sign of hope. (Martin 104)

Paul groans not from excruciating pain or despair, but from his heart's desire to be clothed with his heavenly garments. The presence of the Holy Spirit provides assurance of what is to come. He is the deposit or down payment (2 Corinthians 5:5; Ephesians 1:14) which indicates more will be provided later, providing hope in the in between of life.

If we think in terms of real estate or purchasing a home, the buyer in this situation is God. He has found the home He desires, you and me, where He will come and make His dwelling. Showing His earnest intent, that He has every intention of purchasing this home and moving in to this house, God provides the down payment in the person of Holy Spirit. We are sealed with the hope that God will come one day and make His full Home in us, and we with Him. But for now, we get a foretaste of future glory, which builds on our anticipation and causes us to groan all the more as we strain forward for the finish line, living with hopeful and even joyful anticipation in this place in between.

The groaning described by the apostle Paul is precisely an indication of the presence of the Spirit in our lives. Without the Holy Spirit, we would groan in despair with nothing to hope for; His presence awakens our longing to be with the Lord and move into a more permanent setting. It awakens hope, allowing us to enjoy the appetizer for what it is: an appetizer. Those who do not have this hope find the appetizer less than fulfilling, with no or little hope of anything else to come. Those without this hope jump from appetizer to appetizer, hoping that the new taste will provide the fulfillment and nourishment to the ever hungry soul. The in between of life tempts us to look for full sustenance from the appetizer, to try and squeeze out all that can be had from it, jumping from one appetizer to another in hopes of finding the main course, all with little or no avail.

Everyone groans in life. There are those who groan out of despair and those who groan out of hope and anticipation. The latter are those the apostle Paul is referring to. Are you groaning with hope or despair? The following graph will help you assess yourself.

Groan of Despair	Groan of Hope
Struggles to enjoy life because of what it is, the appetizer. Frustrated with the appetizer, not satisfied with it, can't believe this is all there is, not sure if there is anything more.	Enjoys life for what it is, the appetizer. Knows there is more and looks forward to the main course.
Because there is no or little hope of the future, the now is seldom enjoyed.	Because of the hope of the future, the now is fully enjoyed.
Uses God or the like to live a better life, manipulative, and self-centered.	Uses life to draw close to God, humble, flexible and controlling other-centered.
Seeking to find the finish line - no or little purpose.	Straining forward in victory at the finish line - knows his/her purpose for existence.

Temporary is Frustrating

Having the privilege to be able to buy a home is a wonderful opportunity for anyone. It is one of the benefits of living in America. There is that sense that you are free to use your money as you wish and establish a home that best fits your personality. Establishing a secure place one can call home is important for us in America as the Promised Land was for the ancient Israelites (Genesis 12:1, 7). We dare say it is important for everyone. There is something wonderful about the feeling of permanence, safety, and love that we associate with the idea of home. Longing to have that place, the so-called white-picket fence dream is a part of the American way.

In Mike's early ministry years, he and his wife spent a great deal of their time moving around. In some ways they felt like vagabond or transient ministers of the Gospel. They moved from their first trailer house, after one month of marriage, into the church parsonage. From there, some two years later, they moved to Southern California where Mike attended graduate school and worked with a church. In their California stay, they moved eight more times in a short seven years. "Temporary" was their middle name. It seemed like no matter where they were, it would not be long before they would need to move due to finances, the ministry, or one of their room-mates leaving. Oh, we neglected to mention, Mike and his wife, Teresa always had people living with them, anywhere from one person up to seven at a time. It was a zoo. There was even a time when Teresa was the only female amongst seven young men (including Mike). Teresa and the house-hold were nicknamed by a friend, "Snow White and the Seven Dwarfs." As crazy as it was, they loved it.

There was something in their hearts that longed for something more permanent and in time, a little more private. In spite of this, they surrendered their dream of ever owning a home to the Lord. Shortly after, they were called to plant a church in Phoenix, Arizona where they were able to buy a home. Not only were they able to buy a home, they were able to buy it new and take part in the blessing of watching them build it. Well, they thought, the journey of temporary is now over. Or, is it?

To begin the process of purchasing a home one needs to fill out all the necessary paper work for the loan and place a deposit, earnest money, to secure the place. This is money that is given to indicate you are fully intending to buy the place, a security pledge if you will.

After they knew they were going to buy the home they were amazed at how everything in the house they were renting took on a new meaning. For example, they left most of their boxes packed and only used what items were necessary. They enjoyed the house (the appetizer in this case) they were renting, but looked forward to the home that was being built, groaning with hope for the main course.

They would take drives out to the lot and stand on it and imagine what it would look like, greeted by hope and joy, their new companions. The building process was to take about three and one half months; and so they waited patiently with joy and anticipation. Each week the house progressed a little further and the signs of their moving in were becoming more and more clear.

One of the lessons they learned better than any other is the reality of what the temporary life is like. It felt good to finally move in to their new home and unpack their boxes. To be able to settle in and enjoy the sense of permanence (at least for now) is something they enjoyed to the full.

Maybe that is a perfect picture of our lives. We live in this state of temporary or as we have been calling it, in between. If we have the hope of Christ, then we know there is a more permanent dwelling being built for us, the hope of heaven, and the promise of life with Christ in full. If we have this hope, then this life is somewhat temporary. We might even be able to enjoy our rental house, even decorating it, and making it home while we journey through the in between. What makes life difficult for us, causing us to groan with despair, is when we try and make permanent what is temporary.

Temporary Housing

The apostle Paul makes a clear contrast between what is of preliminary significance and what is of absolute significance. This contrast is expressed in 2 Corinthians 4:16 - 5:5 in various ways. First of all, Paul expresses the distinction between what is permanent and temporary. He writes:

> Therefore we do not lose heart. Though outwardly we are wasting away, yet inwardly we are being renewed day by day. For our light and momentary troubles are achieving for us an eternal glory that far outweighs them all. So we fix our eyes not on what is seen, but on what is unseen. For what is seen is temporary, but what is unseen is eternal. (2 Corinthians 4:16-18 NIV)

The apostle contrasts the appetizer with the main entrée, that which is eternal. When we find ourselves living in between we tend to focus on what is temporary and not what is eternal.

Temporary Housing	**Permanent Dwelling**
(Appetizer)	*(Main Entrée)*
Outer	Inner (2 Corinthians 4:16)
Momentary	Eternal (4:17)
Light or trifling	Weight or abundance (4:17)
Seen	Not seen (4:18)
Temporary	Eternal (4:18)
Earthly	Heavenly (5:1-2)
Tent-like house	Building from God (5:1)
Destroyed	Eternal (5:1)
Naked	Clothed (5:2-4)
Mortality	Life(5:4)

Paul is making the distinction quite clear to the Corinthian congregation the drastic difference between what is earthly and what is heavenly. He is not presenting a dualism whereby the flesh is considered evil or the present life is worth nothing, but simply pointing out that we are built for something more permanent than what this life offers. A house is being built, if you will, and we are living in a rental with our boxes packed and hearts full of anticipation for the glorious day to come when we can move in and unpack forever. The reality of in between only heightens this expectation for us, helping us trust all the more the One who makes the promise, allowing His presence to be our strength (Philippians 4:13).

The apostle reiterates his confidence, the reason why he does not lose heart in 2 Corinthians 5:1 is, as he boldly asserts, that God is building something far better than the temporary earthly tent we have. The main course is still coming. In the previous section, the apostle has been explaining his ministry, particularly the suffering and difficulty he has encountered. (Maybe it would be more correct to say, defending his apostleship to a rather anti-Paul congregation in Corinth.) The apostle has boldly asserted the solution to his dilemma, "we have this treasure in jars of clay to show that this all-surpassing power is from God and not from us" (2 Corinthians 4:7 NIV). He does not try to explain away the pain and suffering, the waiting for the promise, to find its fulfillment. Instead, he focuses on The Promise, the main entrée, the full deal, fixing his eyes on what was not seen, eternal and not on what was temporary or earthly. Maybe that is the problem for us as we journey through the in between of life; that our focus is not on the One who promises, or on what is eternal, but on what is temporary. If there was anyone who understood the in between and knew how to navigate through it; it was the apostle Paul.

We move into chapter 5 of 2 Corinthians with a clear delineation between what is eternal and temporary; what is seen is temporary and what is not seen is eternal. "Tent-like house" is not used apart from this passage by Paul, even though he is a tent-maker by trade (Acts 18:3). Since the time of Pythagoras and Plato, the Greek philosophers often portrayed the physical body as a tent, temporarily inhabited by the soul. The apostle is suggesting that something better awaits those who share in his apostolic faith. As such, he is attempting to give meaning to the present situation by pointing them to the future. It might be good to repeat that line again! Paul is attempting to give meaning to the present by pointing them to the future. This thought might have tremendous bearing on how we can find fullness, joy, and peace as we journey through the in between. In simple language, he is giving them the ultimate thing for which we live - God and His eternal Kingdom.

What we learn from the apostle Paul is that this life is full of instability and vulnerability ("tent-like" and "earthen pots" speaks to this). There is a sense of homelessness we all feel. It's almost as if something tells us we are not where we are supposed to be.

Second, we groan and are burdened in this life as we wait for the new building of God. This is not a groan of despair but of hope. Our ultimate desire is to be with the Lord, enjoying the fullness of life, love, and relationship we were originally created for, much like Mike and Teresa, who waited for their new home to be built, groaning for the day to move in. In their waiting, they were filled with hope and anticipation, never settling for the rental as the permanent dwelling. Why could they do this? Because of the hope Mike and Teresa had in the builder who made the promise to build the home. Like Paul points out in 2 Corinthians 5:1, we can have that same hope in the ultimate Builder, God (The object of "we have" in verse 1 is the hope that a house is being prepared, also reference John 14:2).

Third, what is implied in our text is that we earth dwellers tend to make this life our permanent dwelling when it is not. This life is the rental or the appetizer. It is not the main entrée. In the case of Mike and Teresa, it would have been foolish for them to begin to settle into their rental home and invest money into it, all the while knowing that they would be leaving in the near future for something permanent and far better. As a matter of fact, knowing that they would be leaving made it all the more difficult to settle into their rental house. Their choices were based on their future home; their actions, like leaving most of their boxes packed, were determined by the move they were going to make in the next few months; how they spent their money was geared towards their future house. More simply, their entire life was contingent upon the reality of the more permanent home and not the rental, on the main course and not the appetizer.

Fourth, God has created us for something more permanent, eternal, and has given us the Holy Spirit as a deposit to guarantee His intention toward us (2 Corinthians 5:5). The Holy Spirit is God's cash down, letting us know that He is serious about establishing that permanent dwelling with us in eternity. The basis for Paul's assurance of the permanent triumphing over the temporary is found in the "pledge" or "deposit" (Greek, "arrabon") given to those who place their trust in Christ. God gave Himself to be enjoyed in the now (the appetizer), as well as offering us the assurance that something more still awaits us (the main entrée, the hope realized when we see him face to face as in 1 Corinthians 13:12, also reference 1 John 3:2). As a result of this confidence, Paul does not allow himself to despair (2 Corinthians 4:8). R.V.G. Tasker makes this poignant comment: "Despair is an experience to which he [Paul] does not submit; for to despair is to disown the Spirit and disown the Spirit is not to be a Christian at all" (quoted in Martin 109).

Fifth, as believer's we are guided not by what is seen but by what is not seen (2 Corinthians 4:18). The crucial issue for the apostle is the orientation of one's life.

Sixth, "The issue is not one's present place of residence but what one gives as one's 'home address', what place claims one's loyalty, where one longs to go" (Furnish 303). Even though Mike and Teresa were still living in their rental home while their house was being built, it did not claim their hearts as home nor was it the place they were using for their permanent address. Their mindset was: "We live in Glendale now, but our home will be in Goodyear." In Mike and Teresa's minds, they were already on the road to their new home, just not quite there yet. This sounds like the journey many of us find ourselves on.

Since we have the Spirit as a pledge or down payment, our sole objective is to orient our lives around the Kingdom of God, loving God with all our hearts, loving our neighbor as ourselves and making disciples as we go. This idea of orientation, motion forward, is powerfully expressed in Paul's letter to the Philippians when he writes, "forgetting what lies behind and straining forward to what lies ahead" (Philippians 3:13 RSV). What are you moving toward? What is your address? Are you planning your life around a rental? Or are you living for your future, enjoying the appetizer, but eagerly anticipating the main course?

We have no complaints about the appetizer. It is downright tasty. We have just come to accept the reality (maybe "accepting" is a better word) that life is the appetizer and the main entrée is still coming. What a dish it must be! God has given us so many delights to enjoy here, namely His presence, His promise, and His peace, that to enjoy God in fullness, being with God face to face and partaking of heaven's delicacies in fullness is beyond human description. One day the now will give way to the not yet when the Kingdom of God will come in fullness and all of God's created order in Christ will participate in this fullness as was originally designed.

SECTION THREE

Where Your Treasure Is

But seek first the kingdom of God and his righteousness, and all these things will be added to you. Therefore do not be anxious about tomorrow, for tomorrow will be anxious for itself. Sufficient for the day is its own trouble. (Matthew 6:33-34)

CHAPTER TEN

Your Perspective on Life: "Hotel or Prison"

> Where I live is less the physical place I find myself than the way I perceive my situation (source unknown).
>
> If you think of this world as a place intended simply for our happiness, you find it quite intolerable: think of it as a place of training and correction and it's not so bad. Imagine a set of people all living in the same building. Half of them think it is a hotel, the other half think it is a prison. Those who think it a hotel might regard it as quite intolerable, and those who thought it was a prison might decide that it was really surprisingly comfortable. So that what seems the ugly doctrine is one that comforts and strengthens you in the end. The people who try to hold an optimistic view of this world would become pessimists: the people who hold a pretty stern view of it become optimistic. (quoted in Martindale and Root 279)
>
> You cannot make me feel insecure or bad about myself without my consent (source unknown).

Since the Fall, the universal lot of humankind can best be described as fear. The reality of being separated from God via sin has left an indubitable mark on humanity's core. We are no longer connected to our Creator in the manner we were fashioned, so the state of homelessness or lost-ness is a dominant aspect in the arena of human engagement. Emil Brunner has defined fear as a sense of lost-ness. He writes:

> Fear is the feeling of not being at home, of feeling uncanny and lost in the universe. This fear dominates the life of man, not only exceptionally and in certain individuals who have a tendency that way, but absolutely, and in all human beings at every age. Fear is the air which man-in so far as he is separated from God-breathes, or does not breathe. Fear is the difficulty of breathing-angustiae-the suffocating distress which the soul feels in its separation from God. (Brunner 195)

There is a vague sense, not recognized or admitted by all, in every person of disconnectedness and a longing to find relief for this constant ache of not being fulfilled. Underlying this need for connectedness is a fear that does not want exposure at any level within the soul. As we have made clear, not all people will admit to being afraid but their actions indicate that such is the case. For example, the intense striving for security is really nothing more than an attempt to calm the fear, somehow convincing the mind that everything is ok. Practically speaking, the common attitude of humanity is anxiety, the natural outworking or cousin of fear. Is not anxiety really anything more than the fear of life seeking some form of security? However, no matter how hard we try to secure our lives here on earth, death is still the ultimate outcome. That is an incredibly happy statement.

It appears that many fear life itself; that is, facing the reality in which we become emotionally aware of our state of hopelessness. Like Neo, in the movie *The Matrix*, waking up to the reality that the splinter in our mind was actually making us painfully aware that, what we have come to accept as reality, may not really be all there is. Another way of saying life is empty, or without meaning or purpose, is found in two words - being bored. What this idea describes is the futility and sterility of life and just how empty our souls really are. It seems that people are not too fond of facing the truth of their empty souls, acknowledging the truth the splinter in our minds has awakened us to.

Furthermore, this emptiness or internal boredom is manifested quite acutely in the phrase "to kill time." What an interesting phrase we have crafted for conversation in America, one that seems to be less often utilized in our hurried and over stressed culture where time has become as precious a commodity as gold. And yet, in spite of this lack of time, when we do have some to spare, we find the phrase is articulated by people who are so completely unaware of the tension they feel in life they are allowing something so fundamental as time pass them by, even kill it. That's like looking at the appetizer or only looking at pictures of the appetizer in life's menu without ever sinking your teeth into it.

Let us explain that time is a basic component to life, a substratum of human existence, if you will. It is, essentially, a fundamental element of the known universe, the very element we are wishing to kill.

During the in between of life where patience runs thin and faith often wanes, we are most tempted to seek out this narcotic that can dupe the soul. People will often do anything except allow themselves to experience the pain and frustration of life, especially life in between.

Again, as Augustine stated, "our hearts find no peace until they rest in you" (21). To not understand this aspect of life is to find oneself helplessly wandering around in the labyrinth of the soul. It is precisely this labyrinth that Israel found herself in, hopeful of the Promised Land, and yet caught in the vortex of in between, frustrated and confused as to how they will exactly take the land they have been allowed to see. The obstacles (the giants in this case, Numbers 13:33) to the promise coming to pass seemed overwhelming. To the Book of Numbers we now turn.

A Quick Overview of the Book of Numbers

It is important for us to have a broader understanding of the life situation of the people before we dive into the specifics of our text. The Israelites left Egypt on the fifteenth day of the first month as is noted in Numbers 33:3 (also reference Exodus 12:2) and reached the wilderness of Sinai on the "third new moon" (the first day of the third month) of that same year. Following this, the tabernacle was erected on the first day of the first month in the second year (Exodus 40:17). This is where we pick up our book which starts "on the first day of the second month, in the second year after they had come out of the land of Egypt" (Numbers 1:1). In the same month of that second year the cloud had lifted from the "tabernacle of the testimony" on the twentieth and led the people of Israel on the journey from the wilderness of Sinai to the wilderness of Paran (Numbers 10:11). If we flip over to the book of Deuteronomy, we will find a reference to the "fortieth year, on the first day of the eleventh month" (1:3); suggesting the period the book of Numbers covers is about 38 years.

The book of Numbers fills in quite nicely the period between the Exodus and the Sinai revelation, to the preparations in Moab to enter the Promised Land. The length of the wilderness wandering is also explained by the book. A forty year journey to travel such a short distance is mind boggling. To help us put this in perspective, the Sinai Peninsula is 150 miles across at the top and 260 miles along the sides. The total area is 60,115 sq. km. or 23,220 sq. miles. According to Deuteronomy 1:2, it was only an eleven day journey from Horeb by way of Mount Seir to Kadesh-barnea. No doubt the direct route would have been a few days less, at the most a few weeks if one took the route through Edom and Moab. A comparison of Numbers and Deuteronomy reveals it took about six months for the Israelites to make this trek.

The Book of Numbers is more than mere history. It records the very acts of God. In this respect, it is a rather delicate and complex story of how a relationship can be broken highlighting Israel's unfaithfulness, apostasy, unbelief, disaffection, rebellion, and sheer frustration, set against the backdrop of God's unfailing love and patience. Enough of the biblical history lesson, let's move on to the story in Numbers 13.

The Twelve Spies and Two Opinions: "We can!" and "No, we can't"

In Numbers 13, we have the story of the twelve spies being sent out as a reconnaissance team to explore the Promised Land of Canaan and bring back a report. They were to go and

> See what the land is like and whether the people who live there are strong or weak, few or many. What kind of land do they live in? Is it good or bad? What kind of towns do they live in? Are they unwalled or fortified? How is the soil? Is it fertile or poor? Are there trees on it or not? Do your best to bring back some of the fruit of the land. (Numbers13:18-20 NIV)

Of the twelve spies, only Caleb and Joshua returned believing they could take the land. The reconnaissance from the other ten spies turned out to be a rather dismal and downright negative report, confirming the unbelief the Israelites already possessed. It appears that living that long in between had resulted in some crusty hearts of disillusionment, despair, and doubt. From a quick reading of the text, we can see the fear of the people became quite evident after the report was given as 13:25-29 seems to indicate. Caleb silences the crowd in verse 30 and boldly affirms the ability of Israel to conquer the land. There were two distinct opinions amongst the company of spies, with the majority locked up in fear.

It was Gilbert K. Chesterton who asserted: "Christianity has not been tried and found wanting; it's been found difficult and not tried." Christianity is not an easy lifestyle, nor is it difficult. On the contrary, the life of a believer is quite impossible and can only be accomplished by the power of the Spirit, much more the case when one is journeying through the flatlands of in between.

There is no doubt the task before Israel of taking the land appeared difficult and slightly impossible. There is no question that life possesses giants and intimidating foes that seem to laugh at our smallness and mock our faith. The ten spies were so intimidated by the people who dwelt in the Promised Land that it affected their perception to the point of seeing themselves as grasshoppers in comparison (verse 33).

Have you ever listened to yourself talk? Or stopped to hear the conversation that is going on inside your head? There is a running monologue in our minds, thoughts that run amuck, coloring our perception of life. King David illustrates this for us as he addresses the discouragement of his soul and speaks back to it. "Why are you downcast, O my soul? Why so disturbed within me? Put your hope in God, for I will yet praise him, my Savior and my God" (Psalm 42:5, 11; 43:5 NIV).

In the passage from Psalms, David indicates there is a conversation taking place inside his head. He responds by speaking back to the negative voice that is telling him he will never make it. He is depressed and struggling for a reason to go on. He addresses this negativity by speaking truth to himself about God and his condition. He does not deny his sadness, but only affirms the truth of his life in God. The Israelites could have done the same, acknowledging the enormity of their task and the size of the Nephilim without measuring their outcome based on their self-perception. Only Caleb and Joshua talk back to their fear and doubt, choosing to perceive the situation through the eyes of faith that was focused squarely on God.

Our minds are so difficult to control. The thoughts we struggle to control appear to come from nowhere and bombard us with relentless force. How does one control this problematic cycle of thinking without simply doing mind control? Is that what scripture advocates, learning to simply find new cognitive patterns and implementing them?

Life is not an easy phenomenon to understand. In other words, people are impacted by more than the events or situations they encounter. We know this sounds rather odd, but reality is not always what happens, but what one perceives is happening. What matters is less what is happening than what is perceived. We will call this "perceived reality."

What the 10 spies perceived was less reality than it was perceived reality. Listen to their words, "We saw the Nephilim there (the descendants of Anak come from the Nephilim). We seemed like grasshoppers *in our own eyes*, and we looked the same to them" (Numbers 13:33). The language is powerful; it reveals that what really dictated their response was not the Nephilim but their view of themselves in contrast to the Nephilim. Notice the wording, "we seemed like grasshoppers in our own eyes, and we looked the same to them" that tells us it was how they viewed themselves that determined their fear response and not the actual situation. It was their perception of reality that informed their actions and emotions. This gave them their opinion - not the view of the enemy, but the view of themselves.

To illustrate, if we lose a loved one by death, the surviving family member usually grieves. We can see then that the death of the loved one (the situation or circumstance) resulted in the living family member experiencing grief and sadness. Suppose the same person died and the living family member despised him. The same situation, the death of that person, would now give way to a whole new set of feelings like joy, relief, satisfaction and/or guilt. We can conclude that the situation or circumstance has less to do with how one responds to the event than does the interpretation of it. We have called this the "S.I.R." theory of cognition and emotion. Let us illustrate:

S = *Situation:* What happens to you.
I = *Interpretation:* How you perceive and interpret the event.
R = *Response:* Emotional outcome based on the interpretation.

If we applied this to the ten spies it would look like this:

S = *Situation:* Reconnaissance mission and report of Canaan.
I = *Interpretation:* Viewed themselves as grasshoppers in their own eyes and then placed that back upon the Nephilim "and so we looked the same to them" (Numbers 13:33).
R = *Response:* Fear, doubt, murmuring, division and rebellion resulting in absolute pandemonium (Numbers 14:1-4).

If we are going to find a way to deal with life and live victoriously, particularly in the in between, then we need to understand how we perceive reality, otherwise we will make the same incorrect decisions in response to our circumstances. The problem may not be reality so much as our perception of it. This is not to suggest that reality is horrific, difficult, or even impossible for many, but to firmly declare that perception is critical to the process, and maybe, the most informative for how our journey ends.

One of the points we gather from the story of the twelve spies is the necessity for all believers, and especially leaders, to stand strong in the midst of opposition and difficulty. Like Joshua and Caleb, we need to assert our trust in God, basing our hope and future in the perception that God provides, and not in the circumstantial reality that we see. Although, we believe the unbelief of the people was already in operation before the negative report, it only added fuel to the smoldering fire of unbelief. It is understandable, given the fear of the ten spies, why the people were afraid. Hence, it is all the more crucial for leaders and brothers and sisters to stand together during the trials of life.

With that said, we list some practical points that might assist in facing the giants of our life.

The first thing we see as the result of giving in to fear is an *affected perception*. Notice the line, "we seemed like grasshoppers in our eyes, and we looked the same to them." (13:33 NIV) Fear creates a sense of helplessness: "Then all the congregation raised a loud cry; and the people wept that night" (14:1 NIV). They were afraid they would never be able to have the Promised Land. Hopelessness filled their souls and tainted every action that followed.

Fear leads to murmuring, blaming God, and ascribing a cruel motive to God. The text reads:

> All the Israelites grumbled against Moses and Aaron, and the whole assembly said to them, 'If only we had died in Egypt! Or in this desert! Why is the LORD bringing us to this land only to let us fall by the sword? Our wives and children will be taken as plunder. Wouldn't it be better for us to go back to Egypt?'" (14:2-3 NIV)

Not only is God challenged, but so are His leaders. Fear allows the seed of doubt to germinate, giving way to suspicion and division. Uncaring motives and incompetence are attributed to the leaders, setting the stage for disaffection, switching allegiance.

The people then decide to select another leader. "And they said to each other, 'We should choose a leader and go back to Egypt" (14:4 NIV) We can see that fear gives birth to the desire to find another leader or movement that will calm the storm of emotion within and provide quick relief. Instead of dealing with the problem and embracing the promise, Israel chooses to lay blame on their leaders and run to someone or something else that might provide the narcotic that will dupe the soul. There is nothing like pain that will motivate a person to find an immediate solution.

The bottom line is this: If we succumb to fear, the inevitable result is defeat and further separation from God

Overcoming Fear

We have already stated the common lot of humanity involves fear. If you recall, the sin of the garden left a mark of fear upon the first couple; they now had something to hide, their nakedness or that which is most shameful to us. It is at this point of our earthly existence that the state of disconnectedness or homelessness begins; humanity is lost in the universe of life. We no longer feel at home. The main course, the entrée, has been reserved for later and life has been turned into an appetizer.

As the human story continues, we see the first couple unwilling to give God first place in their lives. Self-protection begins to be the dominant force in their decisions. More appropriately, they are not willing to take responsibility for their act of disobedience, blaming each other and, ultimately, blaming God. Reality is quickly ignored by the first couple, a narcotic of blaming someone else is taken to deaden the pain of life, and the process of denial and fear is firmly set into our human DNA.

With this, the human race now finds itself in the precarious condition we call life, feeling quite ill-equipped to deal with it, unsure of what is really real, as the nagging splinter of our minds ever so quietly reminds us. How then does one overcome fear in the midst of such disconnection?

We suggest that the key to understanding the nature of humanity is found in a word most human beings despise with a vengeance: *dependence*. We are called to be image-bearers or mirrors, bearing and reflecting the image of God in us. We do this most clearly by fulfilling the two basic commands, better called the two great relationships, of loving God with all our heart and our neighbor as our self (Mark 12:30-31). The apostle Paul adds that we are called to reflect God's glory as mirrors or lesser lights as

> all of us have had that veil removed so that we can be mirrors that brightly reflect the glory of the Lord. And as the Spirit of the Lord works within us, we become more and more like him and reflect his glory even more. (2 Corinthians 3:18 NLT)

Mirrors can only reflect that which they behold.

Bear with us as we illustrate. There is only one sun in our solar system and we are not it. Nicolaus Copernicus (1473-1543) changed the way we view our universe and our planet. Up until that time, the Ptolemaic view was the standard view of the day, including that of the philosophers, the church and mainline science. This view held that the earth was the center of the universe, meaning the sun and the planets orbited around the earth. Copernicus came along and reversed this by postulating that the sun was the center of our universe (the principle of heliocentric planetary motion). All of this to say, we are not the center of the universe. The image does not originate in us, we bear the image of God, reflecting His glory, not our own. This universe or world is not about me. This is a critical concept to grasp if we are going to understand what worshiping God really involves.

Like the moon, we are lesser orbs, orbiting around the sun, revealing its brilliant light. The light we have is not our own, but the light of the sun. And in the same way, we are reflecting the light of our Lord, the Son, who is at the center of life's universe. We are mirrors, reflecting the brilliance of our God.

So often in our lives, we reflect ourselves and not the Creator we were designed to reflect. Can you imagine a mirror reflecting something other than what it was beholding? You know, an egotistical mirror. How about an insecure mirror that says, "What if I blow it and don't reflect properly? Besides, have you seen the blemishes on my surface?" This sounds rather silly, doesn't it, and yet, we mirrors seem to specialize in this.

We are God's mirrors - created beings that were fashioned in His image to reflect His glory. We are not the sun, but the moon and can only reflect the light that we have received. That is exactly what it means to be dependent. We are not able to be our own light source, but only able to reflect the light we have received. It is time we turn off our self-made, high-powered generators (broken cisterns as Jeremiah would call them), face the dark reality that will result, embrace the truth that we cannot maintain life in full with God's principles while we ignore our relationship with Him, and trust His presence in the in between of life, letting Him light our world as He sustains us with His presence and life in a way that nothing else can (Acts 17:28).

We are appreciated, valued, and loved dearly by God, but we are not central to life and the universe. This is the first mistake we make as we attempt to live at the center of the universe. In simple language, God does not exist to make us happy or to make a big deal out of us. We exist to bring Him pleasure and to make a big deal out of Him. Creation, the universe, is about Him. Again, this life is not about you or me, but all about God. We are in God's house and the principles implemented for order in the house are His. Understanding our place in the universe is critical for navigating through the in between.

The prophet Isaiah graphically portrays the real struggle of what is transpiring in the daily grind of human existence. The prophet provides one of the clearest pictures of the ongoing struggle we all face.

> Who among you fears the LORD
> and obeys the word of his servant?
> Let him who walks in the dark,
> who has no light,
> trust in the name of the LORD
> and rely on his God.
> But now, all you who light fires
> and provide yourselves with flaming torches,
> go, walk in the light of your fires
> and of the torches you have set ablaze.
> This is what you shall receive from my hand;
> You will lie down in torment. (Isaiah 50:10-11 NIV)

There it is -- the key to overcoming fear. That's right, face your fear, engage and embrace the darkness on purpose by blowing out your torch and walking in the dark. Can we get a "hallelujah"? We can hear the hearts of the faithful respond: "Oh joy! You are saying all we have to do is blow out our torch, walk in the dark blindly, and make it that much easier for the giants (our fear and worst nightmare) in our lives to simply devour us. Excuse me! You've got to be kidding!"

"Ok, Tom and Mike, there is only one thing I don't like about this idea. Walking in the dark is dangerous and can result in harm. I would never tell my kids to do this and God surely would not be telling me to do it!"

God is a loving Father and would not want to intentionally bring harm to His children for harm's sake. No matter how well Neo might have thought he could see in the matrix, it was clear that he was blind to what was really reality. Blowing out our torches allows us to break the power of the matrix and see reality for what it truly is.

Hold tight and let us take you on a journey that just might bring freedom and fullness to your life, but it will involve a direction that you are most likely not going to want to take. Let us suggest a few core concepts to you before we continue:

What we realize in our resistance phase of not wanting to blow out the torch is that we are bent to self. It is not enough to admit you are afraid. You must be willing to walk right into the midst of your fear, face it (Genesis 3:10, Adam admits he is afraid but does not face it), and become dependent upon the mercy of God. Instead of being dependent upon God, we opt for independence by trying to control God somehow (e.g. spiritual disciplines or the like).

Mike played quarterback for his high school football team. During his junior year, they played a team that was out-of-state. It was a high school in Wells, Nevada. Mike's coach talked all week about how big they grew them in Nevada, how quick, how strong, and how determined this Wells team was to be. As the coach talked up Wells, Mike and his team developed an image of the team that was larger than life. They were afraid because of the way the coach made the team sound. As Mike's team entered the field that day, they were met with a reality that only confirmed their fear. Wells was big, had the swagger of confidence, and looked invincible.

The first set of downs for Mike's team suggested this was going to be a long day as the first three of Mike's passes were batted down by the Wells lineman. And yet, as intimidated as Mike's team was they would not quit and by halftime were leading 26 to nothing. Facing our fears or giants is not always as bad as we think as is blowing out our torch. It just might be the pathway to a victorious life in Christ as we journey in between.

Faith is more than believing for changes in our circumstances, it is believing that He exists, and that He is the rewarder of those who diligently seek Him (Hebrews 11:6). It is trusting in the One who gives the promise more than in the promise itself. We think what most people are afraid of is that things will never work out or get better. We tend to find it difficult to trust God with our lives, especially when things are falling apart, because we do not really believe He will provide. This leads us to take over the control center of our hearts and assume the position of God in our lives. If we turn back to Numbers 14:2-3, we see the people's fear involves dying and not having a place to call home. They were crying out for security. We must realize that dependency is not learned apart from being broken (not wounded but broken, submitted, soft like clay) and made to realize we are created as dependent beings.

It's ok to be afraid and insecure. We all are. Ok, just take a moment and admit it. Relax, there is no one around. Say it, "I am afraid. I am insecure." If you find yourself not able to say it well then try this: "I cannot control life or the outcome of life." Unlike Captain Kirk of Star Trek's Enterprise you cannot cheat death or change the rules of life to overcome life's Kobayashi Maru (a "no-win" scenario test to evaluate potential commanders). Truth in life is not stable and we cannot control it. Allow yourself to take a dose of reality today and face the imperfection of life and face the darkness we all really live in (i.e., the matrix).

Tom lived for a number of years after his Cystic Fibrosis diagnosis with a physical sense of insecurity, wondering at times "what's next" for him as he faced CF. Born with this condition, there was no control possible on his part: He could not go back and somehow undo his genetic code. Peace came to him through releasing control of the situation to the Lord. He figured that if he had been kept alive by the Father this long, He would see Tom through the balance of his days. So, beyond his normal daily healthcare routine, which is rather taxing in-and-of itself, Tom has released the issue to the Lord. However, he is still looking forward to that day he does see Jesus, as he wants the "upgrade" referred to in 1 Corinthians 15, what Tom humorously refers to as Body 2.0. Tom accepts his health situation, while still contending for health and healing, but fixes his eye on eternity rather than this life now.

We all long for more, for the perfect, but until we can admit that every human endeavor or relationship is somewhat less than what we expected, we will never be able to face the reality of life (reference Romans 8:18-25, "we groan inwardly"). Too often, when we pray for the leading of the Spirit, we are actually praying for a no-anguish life. We are not suggesting that such a prayer is wrong, but that we are praying for our agenda and not God's.

As we have already noted, as fallen creatures we are bent to the self, so much so that God has to bring us to places of brokenness and longing before we will ever admit to our need for Him. God humbles us so that we might come to a point of recognizing we need Him; so that we might become dependent upon Him.

Even King David admits to the depression of life in Psalms 42 and 43.

We must learn to challenge our perceptions - renewing the mind. The battlefield of life is the mind, where the matrix can be constructed ever so subtly. Our perceptions of God, life, ourselves, and others are often distorted. Once the perception is distorted, that is how we come to view reality. "We seemed to ourselves like grasshoppers, and so we seemed to them." The way we view life is the way life will be to us, but not necessarily the way life really is.

In high school Mike was insecure and wanted everyone to like him, but believed they really did not. This resulted in his inability to stand up for his faith in Christ. He perceived people viewed him as a religious idiot and freak. Bob was someone who intimidated Mike in his high school years because he was the cool party man. He was not able to stand up to him until his 10 year reunion when Bob proceeded to use the same party language and encourage Mike to engage and drink-away. Mike was able to graciously decline and share His life in Jesus with Bob. At that stage in Mike's life, he no longer viewed himself as a grasshopper in his own eyes, nor to Bob anymore.

Practice reality checks with the Lord and remind yourself that God is with you (Deuteronomy 31:6). Dependence upon the Lord involves obedience to His ways and constantly remembering the things He has done for us. If we forget the things of God we will find ourselves moving into independence and fear. To stay close to God, remembering His power, leaning upon His strength, is to stay in a place of security and dependence.

Abandon your life to God and to loving His people and you will find your life fulfilled. Take control of the only thing you can, your attitude and response to situations. This is essential in reorienting your thinking and the renewing of your mind. Until the Kingdom becomes your priority, you will continue to be dazed and confused, reacting rather than responding to the things you encounter in this life.

"I will come and proclaim your mighty acts, O Sovereign LORD; I will proclaim your righteousness, yours alone" (Psalm 71:16).

Hotel or Prison

Let's refresh our minds with the quote from C. S. Lewis that we cited at the beginning of the chapter. Lewis said,

> If you think of this world as a place intended simply for our happiness, you find it quite intolerable: think of it as a place of training and correction and it's not so bad. Imagine a set of people all living in the same building. Half of them think it is a hotel, the other half think it is a prison. Those who think it a hotel might regard it as quite intolerable, and those who thought it was a prison might decide that it was really surprisingly comfortable. So that what seems the ugly doctrine is one that comforts and strengthens you in the end. The people who try to hold an optimistic view of this world would become pessimists: the people who hold a pretty stern view of it become optimistic. (quoted in Martindale and Root 279)

This life will be for you what you perceive it to be, a hotel or a prison. You choose! Your spirit and your mind have been freed to perceive the true reality around you. Through the scriptures illuminated by the Holy Spirit, and by the Spirit's loving voice, the Living Word of Christ in you, you can see and know what the truth of your reality is. Embrace it, as painful as it may be, so that you can overcome and gain the mind of Christ. This world is not our home. We look for a better country, and yet this world is not our prison. It is simply our temporary dwelling for those who are truly not of this world.

CHAPTER ELEVEN

Overcoming: "Living in the Land of In Between's"

We see in our story line that for life to be lived it must be at great risk, as is the case in Genesis 39, the story of Joseph. Life must be lived in the face of deceit, temptation, and seduction. Not only are evils of all kind all around, but so are tempting ways of life like self-security, the way of the Egyptian empire. Joseph had an ample opportunity to be his own source of strength and security. Instead, he chose righteousness and to be loyal to God.

In Genesis 39:1-6 and 21-23, because God's favor was upon Joseph, we see that the things of his life are "confidently settled". There is no room for incongruities or abrasions here; God brings to pass what He planned. The Egyptian empire will submit to God's will. Things in our lives are confidently settled because of the stability of the person of God (James 1:17). His will for us and for our lives cannot be shaken or overthrown. Consequently our hearts can be confidently settled in that God is able to bring to pass His good, pleasing and perfect will for our lives.

In order for us to grasp the essence of Joseph's story effectively, we must embrace the tension within both truths: *life must be lived with great risk and; things are confidently settled.* If we take either truth without the other we run the risk of oversimplifying life. Both slices of bread are necessary for the sandwich of life to be enjoyed properly. Joseph's story, much like our own stories, struggles with real life and real faith. We can experience God and experience life; our narrative assumes the essential compatibility of both.

If you are prone to live in the extreme of religious affirmation (the "promise only" people) then you probably won't make it past verse 6. Life can't go wrong for you and when it does, you do all you can to believe and pray it back to the "things are confidently settled" stage. More simply, these are people who are interested only in the promise and miss the reality of life.

On the other hand, if you live in the extreme of "life is risk," then you might find yourself living only in verses 7-20 of Genesis 39. Life is more than taking action and doing things. We are not the masters of our destiny. No matter what the world tells you, you cannot simply decide your future without the other slice of bread; *things are confidently settled by God.* Our text is dealing with a kind of humanity, which fully relies on God and fully engages in life. It is the balancing act of tension, living the in between that the human heart would rather not experience.

Joseph's suffering makes sense in the midst of the promise. For the promise to take place, the situations had to be orchestrated as they were. For him to meet the cupbearer and interpret his dreams, he needed to be in the royal prison in a position of favor. God maneuvered the elements so that this could take place. As Joseph managed Potiphar's house, God was preparing him to rule Egypt. Joseph's present disgrace is then a preliminary step to his future glory. This is more adequately expressed in simple language by the apostle Peter as he writes: "Humble yourselves…under the mighty hand of God so that at the proper time he may exalt you" (1 Peter 5:6).

The key to living in the land of in between is obedience. The life of Joseph clearly models righteousness in spite of what was happening to him. *The avenue for his blessing was through the obedient act.* We find it interesting that Joseph continues to live a righteous life even though his journey appears to be taking him further and further away from the promise. There is something in the response of submission that is central to God's work in us. *Obedience and submission position us to receive from the Lord.* Tom, in his dealing with life with Cystic Fibrosis, makes his goal by simply being obedient to Jesus each day. If he focuses on this, he knows he will be able to be effectively used by his loving Father in Kingdom work. How long, he does not know, nor does he overly concern himself with that issue any longer. What Tom does know is that while he is walking this earth, he will seek to allow the Father to work in him to make him the son He desires him to be; and to work through him in Kingdom collaboration. Such a position puts Tom in God's path of life and blessing. Here is another illustration of this point:

> Many times certain situations evolve to a point that we have to step aside. To walk out of it is a real act of faith since I get the feeling at such times that I must attend to the outcome of my problems or they will never get solved. But the truth seems to be that I am like

> my little girl who was continually picking the scab off a wound to see if it had healed. There is a sense in which I reach a point at which I have looked at my situation until any more direct attention to it, even in prayer, becomes a step away from Christ. I have to walk away in raw faith believing that God will work beneath the scab. (Keith Miller)

We must not allow ourselves to be caught up in the self-serving trap of our own need-meeting. We must trust God to supply all things, and always in His timing.

Calculation or Trust

Living in between tends to reveal what is at the heart of an individual. Our life's orientation, what we are living for, what or who we truly trust, and the real status of our relationship with God is made ever so clear in the in between.

When we find ourselves waiting on the promise we tend to fall into two simple categories of *calculating* and *trusting*. The calculator sizes up the situation only to fall prey to discouragement once the raw data is processed, because the data only makes certain the situation is impossible. This is a person who is constantly calculating and figuring out what it would take for the provision to come, consistently proving how impossible it is for the miracle to happen. This person knows what it will take, but is trapped in only seeing the situation from a human perspective and not God's.

The person who fits this description is the apostle Philip (the Calculating One). We meet Philip in this posture in John 6, where Jesus has the crowds sit down and asks Philip, "Where shall we buy bread for these people to eat?" (John 6:5b NIV). Philip provides no solution, but only magnifies the problem as he responds, "'Eight months' wages would not buy enough bread for each one to have a bite!" (John 6:7 NIV). Simply, "after calculating the situation Master, there is no way we can do this. We are doomed!"

The second is the one who trusts and brings what he has to Jesus. This person is most clearly seen in the life of the apostle Andrew, the one who brings his stuff to Jesus and trusts Him with it. This is a person who, even in the throes of impossibility, is looking to bring to Jesus what he has or can find. Although Andrew demonstrated faith and willingness, he is still not quite aware of what Jesus will do. All he knows is that he had better bring the Master something. This fascinates us because the text simply says the

Master asked Philip. There is no hint of a request to go and get food. It appears the stuff of this provision is that brought by Andrew. This is an interesting thought. Is it possible that our provision is only an obedient and trusting act away?

It's Time to Overcome

So, how then do you step out in faith (living life with great risk) all the while believing that God has everything under control (that things are confidently settled)? How does one obey, trusting God, yet without being calculating? How do we inherit His promises while living in the midst of a reality that is confusing, where there is little definition and so much ambiguity? How do we live without cutting a deal with the Devil and settling for less than God's best intention? How do we live in this life looking to the future perfect of the Kingdom that is not yet, while not embracing the denial in which so many choose to live? How do we embrace the now of the Kingdom, without creating a system of belief through which we manipulate and control God? How can we enjoy having the appetizer of this life, while still looking forward to the full meal deal of eternity? What can we do to live as aliens and sojourners in this world, seeing life on this planet as living in a hotel rather than in a prison?

These questions of how, are the ones we must ask if we are to overcome the in between. There are no pat answers for any of them, no "one size fits all" solution which can be mass produced and applied to every life. Life is tailor-made to fit each one of us, and the answers to each of these questions are likewise shaped to fit each of us individually. Seeking these answers for each of us is part of the in between tension we live in. There are no easy answers, but rather an ongoing quest within the context of our relationship with our heavenly Father. However, there are certain biblical principles about the overcoming of life's obstacles and inheriting the promises of God that are common to all. While there may be many such principles that relate to victorious living, there are eight we would like to highlight here.

First Principle: There is a God, and you are not Him

While it seems this should not even have to be mentioned here, coming to this realization is a central factor in human redemption, as it is at the core of the fallen human condition. We want existence to be all about us, and to that end we want to control it so that we can shape it to our liking.

For God to change us and transform us we must be willing to relinquish any sense of control we may have. As stated earlier, all control is an illusion; we do not have the power to change the outcomes of life. Jesus makes this clear when He addresses worry, the natural fruit of trying to control.

> And he said to his disciples, "Therefore I tell you, do not be anxious about your life, what you will eat, nor about your body, what you will put on. For life is more than food and the body more than clothing. Consider the ravens: they neither sow nor reap, they have neither storehouse nor barn, and yet God feeds them. Of how much more value are you than the birds! And which of you by being anxious can add a single hour to his span of life? *If then you are not able to do as small a thing as that*, why are you anxious about the rest?" (Luke 12:22-26)

We are not God. We are not in control. Jesus makes it clear from this passage that we cannot do anything to influence our needs being met. The sooner we realize this fact the sooner we are able to receive the transformation which He desires to bring us, a transformation which frees us to embrace living in the now as we look to the not yet, and doing so victoriously and with joy. God is the source of our life in abundance - and we are not God.

Second Principle: Everything in life is about an on-going relationship with God

We know this from the core of our Christian teaching about salvation and life everlasting, but we often fail to realize the need to keep this thought in the forefront of our minds daily. That relationship is key to victory and overcoming. Maintaining our relationship with the Lord and deepening it is required if we are to obtain His promises in this life and the next. The path to the fulfillment of the promises is a Person: Jesus is the Way. The understanding we need to navigate life in between is a person: Jesus is the Truth. The source of our life and hope and joy as we endure the hardships of this part of our existence is a Person: Jesus is the Life (John 14:6). Jesus is the true "Yes" to all of God's promises, they are completed in Him (2 Corinthians 1:20).

His presence is the true promise (Galatians 3:14) - the Spirit of Christ who dwells within us. Without His Spirit there is no redemption, no new birth. Without the Spirit there is no process of sanctification and transformation. Unless the Holy Spirit indwells us, we will not receive a future of resurrection and glorification.

His presence allows us to live in the tension of in between. It is through His indwelling Spirit that we are empowered to stand in spite of circumstances. It is through the presence of His Spirit in us that we can live in the ambiguity of this life, and not need the definition our broken, selfish, controlling nature desires. We can be at peace in the now of the Kingdom with our eyes firmly fixed on the not yet, as we have the Holy Spirit as a guarantee of our inheritance:

> In him you also, when you heard the word of truth, the gospel of your salvation, and believed in him, were sealed with the promised Holy Spirit, who is the guarantee of our inheritance until we acquire possession of it, to the praise of his glory. (Ephesians 1:13-15)

Third Principle: We must realize our need

We can only ask for something if we truly are in need of it. This is the reality behind Jesus' words in Matthew 5:3 - "Blessed are the poor in spirit, for theirs is the kingdom of heaven."

We must come to understand that we are at our best when we are "poor in spirit", dependent on God (Isaiah 40:31), weak in our strength (2 Corinthians 12:9); and fully oriented to the Kingdom of God (Philippians 3:12-14).

In the movie, *Willie Wonka and the Chocolate Factory* with Gene Wilder in the 1970's, there were cute, little people called the "oompah-loompahs." They were the workers of the factory, laboring to make the magical chocolate of Willie Wonka. We, in much the same way, are oompah-loompahs. The oompah-loompahs illustrate for us the real size each of has in relationship to our enemy, the devil. We are really midgets fighting a battle with a Goliath. Our voices are high-pitched and our strength is small. However, it is not the power of the little ones that wins the battle; it is the power of our God. Satan is not overwhelmed by you, but by the Christ that is in you (1 John 4:4).

Those who know their need will receive the Kingdom. The first step to overcoming is to admit your need.

Fourth Principle: We must ask for the Kingdom of God to come

It is not enough simply to realize the need that each of us has for the blessings of God's Kingdom rule in our life. Rather we must live with dependence on God. We must daily acknowledge our need for Him and His rule in our lives. It is daily we must seek Him, His righteousness and His Kingdom to keep the proper attitude of dependence. Heaven forbid that we would slip back into self-reliance (which we all do) and is exactly what Jesus wants to prevent His disciples from doing. This is at the core of what we call the Lord's Prayer. Depending on which tradition within the Christian faith you come from, you may have learned to approach this prayer as either something to be memorized and recited or as a model for one's personal prayer life. While both may have certain validity, embracing either as the totality misses the intent of Jesus' teaching through this prayer. Let's look at this closer.

When asked by His disciples to teach them to pray in Luke 18, Jesus responded not so much by giving them a format, but in opening their minds to the reality of God's Kingdom rule being the source of their life and provision. The means to access that resource was through relationship with a loving heavenly Father (Our Father). That Father was perfect (hallowed be Thy name) and lived in perfection (Who art in heaven). Jesus tells His disciples to pray that perfection into their own reality (come Kingdom of God, be done will of God, here and now, as it already is in perfection). In essence, He is telling them to grab hold of the future-perfect resource of the Kingdom not yet here and pull it to them in the now through prayer. Next He instructs them to lay up food in a heavenly storehouse for tomorrow, that God might dispense it at the point of future need (give us today tomorrow's bread). This is a storehouse beyond their control, one which contains all the provision of the future Kingdom, accessible in the now through trusting a capable Provider. This part of the prayer demonstrates how out of control we really are, and how dependant we are upon God.

This all messes with our fallen human perception of time-space a bit, but nonetheless, Jesus follows along this track as He tells them that they will receive forgiveness in the now based on the forgiveness they have already been given (ask to be forgiven now and in the future, just as you have already been forgiven). Ultimate forgiveness is not handed out to anyone until they stand in the presence of God - in the future of the perfect Kingdom. Time seems to mean nothing to Him.

He wraps up the prayer telling them to ask to be kept from temptation in the future, and delivered from the evil one now. Both of these requests are based in the future perfect of the Kingdom: There will be no temptation and there will be no Evil One! The ability to be delivered from Evil rests in the lordship of Jesus Christ, His Kingdom rule. Likewise, the ability to resist temptation comes from His obedience. In the Kingdom yet to come we will all be perfectly obedient like Jesus and completely free from the Evil One. It is in that, we put our hope and on that, we base our approach to God in prayer. We are asking for a bit of the future perfect of the not yet to come to us here in the now.

Please hear us - *there is no more important functional aspect of living in the land of in between than appropriating this reality, and implementing it in our lives.* Such appropriation of the Kingdom is essential to walking as sojourners. We are in a life which can leave us dazed and confused - but we can have clarity which comes from outside that frame of reference, from a God who is neither affected nor troubled by a fallen nature. We live in a land of spiritual lack, and sometimes in natural want, but we have access to provision for all our needs through a Provider with an infinite storehouse. We live under a dominion of Darkness which is planetary in scale, but are freed from its rulership by allegiance to another King, submitted to His lordship.

To live in this life, we must access the next, drawing on the resources of the Kingdom yet to come, our Promised Land of completely fulfilled promises. It is in this way, through relationship with God (who we are not) and our lifestyle of dependence on Him (lived out through prayer) we can live fruitfully in the in between.

Fifth Principle: We must persist in our asking

There is something about an active faith stance that releases the power of God in our lives and positions us to receive from Him. We must persist: "If you and I are really to obtain these blessings which God has for us, we must go on asking for them" (Lloyd-Jones 200). We must keep in mind,

> Our Lord does not promise to change life for us; He does not promise to remove difficulties and trials and problems and tribulations; He does not say that He is going to cut out all the thorns and leave the roses with their wonderful perfume. No; He faces life realistically, and tells us that these are things to which the flesh is heir, and which are bound to come . . . But He assures us that we can so know Him that, whatever happens, we need never be frightened, we need never be alarmed. (Lloyd-Jones 196)

Each of us, as we walk through the land of in between, will find ourselves at a crossroads in our Christian life where the Spirit of God is giving us a sense of unlimited blessing and life if we will but take Him at His Word and "beat the ground." In 2 Kings 13, the account of Elisha and Jehoash illustrates the practicality regarding God's way of securing victory for us. The king of Israel, Jehoash, comes to Elijah in a moment of crisis crying out, "My father, my father! The chariots of Israel and its horsemen!" (verse 14). Elisha tells him to grab a bow and some arrows and draw the bow with one of the arrows. As the king does this, Elisha places his hands on Jehoash's hands. Following this, he instructs Jehoash to open the east window and shoot one of the arrows.

Here is where the story grabs us with a touch of realism. Not just any arrow, but the "Lord's arrow of victory, the arrow of victory over Aram!" (verse 17 NIV). The only difference between the arrow before and after Jehoash touched it is the hands of the prophet have touched the hands of the king. The narrative does not tell us the arrow changed in any way, shape, or form. As far as we are concerned, the arrow is still just an arrow. However, the prophet sees something we do not, for in the placing of his hands, something happened that now caused the arrow to become the "Lord's arrow of victory." There is something powerful about this detail of the story that transcends time and speaks to us today. When we encounter the obstacles of life, the activity of faith is often focused around things that are nothing more than natural elements. In other words, there is often nothing all that miraculous about the things the Lord tells us to do.

In order for the victory to transpire, Jehoash must believe that it will. As noted earlier, the writer of Hebrews tells us when he writes: "And without faith it is impossible to please God, because anyone who comes to him must believe that he exists and that he rewards those who earnestly seek him" (11:6 NIV). As we have said, there is something about obedience that releases faith. God has, in His sovereignty, decided to work through the vehicle of faith and obedience as the release point of His power. Here we see this truth played out.

The victory the Lord promises Jehoash over Aram is complete. "You will completely destroy the Arameans at Aphek" (2 Kings 13:17b NIV).

The king is then told to strike the ground with the arrows (verse 18) as an act of appropriating the truth via faith. Jehoash took the arrows and only struck the ground three times. He settled for less which quickly brought a rebuke from the man of God. "'You should have struck the ground five or six times; then you would have defeated Aram and completely destroyed it. But now you will defeat it only three times'" (verse 19 NIV).

The measure of victory that we have been given is absolute through the death and resurrection of our Lord. However, the level we experience it in this life has everything to do with how much we are able to appropriate the truth in our daily lives.

We need to be like the "persistent widow" of Jesus' parable in Luke 18, pressing into God until He gives us the Kingdom. Don't be afraid to be a holy irritation to God.

Sixth Principle: Faith is Movement

We need to move! God's provision comes through an act of faith, like we just described. Frederick Buechner says this about faith:

> We must take the shield of faith, and faith here is not so much believing this thing or that about God as it is hearing a voice that says, 'Come unto me.' We hear the voice, and then we start to go without really knowing what to believe about the voice or about ourselves; and yet we go. Faith is standing in the darkness, and a hand is there, and we take it. (*Magnificent Defeat* 42)

Take what you have and let God have it. God will multiply it - provision as we act. *Action is the backdrop to provision.* "So, you see, it is impossible to please God without faith. Anyone who wants to come to him must believe that there is a God and that he rewards those who sincerely seek him" (Hebrews 11:6 NLT). Be active in your faith (ask, seek, and knock) and be persistent!

It is impossible to steer a ship which is tied-up to the dock. For the rudder to work there must be forward motion in the ship and water flowing over the rudder. Forward motion by faith is essential for the Lord to direct us into His path toward His promises.

Seventh Principle: Surrender to God, not the Situation or Circumstance

Surrendering to the Lord and His will for our lives is essential in releasing the stress of walking through this land of in between. It becomes possible to know His will for us - it is not intended to be a mystery - as we allow Him to renew our minds (Romans 12:1-2). As we choose to allow Him to work in us and to conform us to His image, we can realize the purposes and plans He has already made for us (Ephesians 2:10).

Walking in victory in this life requires that we surrender to the instructions of the Lord, following the example of Jesus (John 5:19). We must do whatever the Spirit tells us to do. The quitter says, "To hell with God. If He won't tell me, I'll do it myself." The person who surrenders asks, "Where is the hell in me? What do You want, Lord? Here I am. Speak Lord, your servant listens."

We need to let go. By letting go we are not referring to quitting, being mediocre, or even irresponsible. Rather it means to surrender to God as an act of faith. It is a decision of the will to release our life and allow God to work through us. God does not use us significantly until we take our hands off of our lives and lay them down. Nor can He work in our lives, situations and circumstances if we continue to demand control. (See Principle One.)

We must keep in mind the following dynamic when encountering situations of difficulty. We are not seeking to simply overcome the situation. Rather we are seeking the Lord so that He might increase us to be more like Jesus, to make us larger than the situation. Our desire is to be more pleasing to Him. Victory will flow from a posture that seeks to glorify our Lord in all things. Obedience and submission position us to receive from the Lord.

A blacksmith, about eight years after he had given his heart to God, was approached by an intelligent unbeliever with the question: "Why is it you have so much trouble? I have been watching you. Since you joined the church and began to walk square and seem to love everybody, you have had twice as many trials and accidents as you had before. I thought that when a man gave himself to God his troubles were over. Isn't that what the parsons/preachers tell us?"

With a thoughtful but glowing face, the blacksmith replied: "Do you see this piece of iron? It is for the springs of a carriage. I have been 'tempering' it for some time. To do this I heat it red-hot, and then plunge it into a tube of ice-cold water. This I do many times. If I find it taking 'temper', I heat the hammer unmercifully. In getting the right piece of iron I found several that were too brittle. So I threw them in the scrap pile. Those scraps are worth about a cent a pound; this carriage spring is very valuable."

He paused, and his listener nodded. The blacksmith continued: "God saves us for something more than to have a good time. That's the way I see it. We have a good time all-right, for God's smile means heaven. But He wants us for service just as I want this piece of iron. And He has put the 'temper' of Christ in us by testing us with trials. Ever since I saw this I have been saying to Him, 'Test me in any way you choose, Lord: only don't throw me in the scrap pile.'"

We must stand in the face of adversity, not give in to it or run from it, never surrendering to the circumstance. Rather, we overcome the circumstance by surrendering to God and His perfect will - whatever that may be.

We end this principle with two quotes from Winston Churchill on endurance:

> Never give in, never give in, never; never; never; never - in nothing, great or small, large or petty - never give in except to convictions of honor and good sense.

> Sure I am of this, that you have only to endure to conquer.

Eighth Principle: Realize the Source of the promises

There is a Person behind the promise, God our Father, and we need to develop the practice of giving thanks to Him while we are journeying through the in between. Gratitude and thanksgiving is the stage upon which the acts of God are performed. If we are not thankful to the Person of the promises, it can still become all about us. The promises flow to us out of the relationship we have with our Father, as we discussed earlier, as do both the strength and wisdom to walk in the land of in between. We need to be able to bless His name in all things of this life, the good, the bad and the ugly. A current worship chorus by Matt and Beth Redmond really depicts this attitude well, and could be considered a theme song for living in between:

Blessed Be Your Name
Blessed be Your name
In the land that is plentiful
Where Your streams of abundance flow
Blessed be Your name

Blessed be Your name
When I'm found in the desert place
Though I walk through the wilderness
Blessed be Your name
Every blessing You pour out
I'll turn back to praise
When the darkness closes in
Lord still I will say
Blessed be the name of the Lord

Blessed be Your name
Blessed be the name of the Lord
Blessed be Your glorious name

Blessed be Your name
When the sun's shining down on me
When the world's all as it should be
Blessed be Your name

Blessed be Your name
On the road marked with suffering
Though there's pain in the offering
Blessed be Your name

You give and take away
You give and take away
My heart will choose to say
Lord blessed be Your name

It is the attitude of thankfulness in all things that unrestricts God's hand (His hand is never bound, but our ability to receive can be limited by our lack of obedience), and it is because of who God is as a person that we can have confidence that the supply never runs out. As Paul says in Philippians 4:19, "And this same God who takes care of me will supply all your needs from his glorious riches, which have been given to us in Christ Jesus" (NLT).

There is one last key to overcoming while living in between: *We must believe that there is such a thing as the abundant life - and that God intends us to have it.* This is the content of our next and final chapter.

CHAPTER TWELVE

This Abundant Life

Settling for Less

Can you imagine winning the chance to shop in a grocery store or clothing store for three minutes and within the time frame you would be able to keep whatever you grabbed. How intense do you think you would be?

What if you found yourself the winner of a car dealership's promotion that allowed you a chance to drive off the lot with as many new cars as you were able? The only catch to the dream is finding the right keys. The dealership has staged the game with a board of keys, some 200 in all, the exact number of cars in the lot, all you have to do is find the key that unlocks the door and starts the car. You have five minutes to run to the board and take as many keys as you can and run to the cars to see if any of them are the right ones. I ask you, how intense would you be?

A true story: A man in Portland, Oregon was passing out free $20.00 bills to people on the sidewalk. He simply wanted to give people some money and so he did. Ironically, he found it slightly difficult to do so. The people were suspicious and thought there was a catch, and many did not take the money. How odd.

Jesus offers us the abundant life and we, oddly enough, do not press Him for it or truly take Him at His Word and appropriate it. If we do accept the possibility of the abundant life, there is a gentle nudge to do so with mediocrity. Most of us settle with the "it's good enough" mentality when it comes to the things of the Kingdom.

It's An Issue of Perspective

Satan's greatest con game is the one in which he gets us to believe for whatever reason that we cannot have the full, abundant life Jesus calls us to live out. Maybe the enemy has successfully moved you to focus on God's prohibition in your life rather than His provision. I suspect that something of the following is what is taking place in our minds:

"It's too good to be true."
"I won't win anyway, so why try?" This translates into "the abundant life is available, but not for me."
"I'll make a fool of myself."
"This is a cruel joke."
"There's just too many cars to choose from."
"What if I don't choose the right one?"

We end up buying a lie and believing God is truly not in the blessing or will strip us of it, so we settle for less when it comes to living for the Kingdom. *After all, it is easier to live with planned disappointment than it is to make one's heart vulnerable to the possibility of being let down.* Allow us to ask some rather penetrating questions.

We will grant you the reality of being dysfunctional and struggling in this life, but when does the reality of the abundant life become a part of our lives as new creatures in Christ with old things passing away and all things becoming new? (2 Corinthians 5:17). Is there not a way to rise above the situations and distressing moments of life? Are we destined to simply struggle our way through without any hope of achieving a sense of victory and joy? What is the peace that Jesus wants to leave with us and does, a peace the world does not give and cannot? (John 14:27) If it is salvation, then why don't we have it flowing out of our lives?

The answer is simple. We have settled for the attitude of "it's good enough." Our perspective becomes, influenced by our negative life experiences - "The abundant life may exist, but my experience indicates otherwise. Therefore, it must not exist for me - so I'll just take what I can get."

The Abundant Life is Real

We quoted Numbers 23:19 earlier - God does not lie. He does not promise and then not perform. No matter what your experience is, God is good, and the abundant life is real. Not an easy life, nor a life free from trouble, but a life that can have righteousness, peace and joy in the Holy Spirit (Romans 14:17). Jesus did come to give you the abundant life He promised you in John 10:10 - in the now of this life as well as the not yet of the future Kingdom. What we often fail to understand is that there is another one, the Enemy of your soul, who seeks to kill you, steal from you and destroy you. It is in the defeat of this Evil One that your abundance lay, and Jesus has already triumphed over him. Now what you must do is continually, on a daily basis, respond to this victory by appropriating what the Lord has won for you. It is through that lifestyle of utter dependence that we lay hold of the Kingdom and its blessings, utter dependence on the King of kings and Lord of lords, the One who rules over all.

No matter what your experience may indicate to you, there is an abundant life. While our fallen nature taints and dulls our spiritual sight, making it difficult to perceive the truth of God's Kingdom and all of its joys and graces, it is real - whether we can see it or not. Only believe, and you shall see.

Jesus Intends for You to Have an Abundant Life

Not only is the abundant life real, but Jesus does intend for you to have it. He didn't suffer, die by crucifixion and be raised from the dead by His Father just so you could have some sort of spiritual retirement home in the Great By-and-By. This is no limitation on His end, and no demon from Hell can stand in the way of your receiving it. He wants to bless you with all things of His Kingdom rule, some of which will be realized in this life, all of which will be realized in the next. This is what Paul was referring to when he wrote the Romans in his great letter, discussing the power of God's love:

> What then shall we say to these things? If God is for us, who can be against us? He who did not spare his own Son but gave him up for us all, how will he not also with him graciously give us all things? Who shall bring any charge against God's elect? It is God who justifies. Who is to condemn? Christ Jesus is the one who died -- more than that, who was raised -- who is at the right hand of God, who indeed is interceding for us. Who shall separate us from the love of Christ? Shall tribulation, or distress, or persecution, or famine, or nakedness, or danger, or sword? As it is written,

"For your sake we are being killed all the day long;
we are regarded as sheep to be slaughtered."

> No, in all these things we are more than conquerors through him who loved us. For I am sure that neither death nor life, nor angels nor rulers, nor things present nor things to come, nor powers, nor height nor depth, nor anything else in all creation, will be able to separate us from the love of God in Christ Jesus our Lord. (Romans 8:31-38)

No, the limitation is on our side, and is usually found in two things, either ignorance of the Kingdom, its dynamics and its blessings, or in a crippling sense of unworthiness - feeling like we don't deserve the Kingdom. We are hoping this book has been helpful in addressing, at least in part, the misunderstanding of the Kingdom and the promises of its King. May the Lord build on any new understanding you may have obtained and release the grace you need to walk with Him in between. The issue of worthiness is different altogether. If you are feeling that the Kingdom experience you have and are having is less than advertised, and this has left you wondering "What about me? What am I-chopped liver?", then you have done just what the Enemy wants - you have believed a lie. You have bought the picture he wants you to have of yourself in relation to God. By the way, the Devil himself doesn't even believe the lies about you. He knows who you are in Christ. His whole goal is to keep you from realizing the truth of who you are. Every time you buy this lie, the matrix is reloaded, over and over, again and again, into your consciousness. You buy into the unreal fabric of doubt, doubting both Christ and who you are in Him, doubting His desire to bless you and His willingness to help you overcome while you are waiting for the fulfillment of His promises.

Just as the reality of the abundant life is true, so this also is true - your loving heavenly Father desires to bless you - and has already done so - with every spiritual blessing in Christ Jesus. It is now for you to seek Him and receive all that you need, holding fast to your hope, looking to receive His great and very precious promises. Along this line, as a closing thought, we would like to share with you a passage of a blessing from the Apostle Paul.

> Blessed be the God and Father of our Lord Jesus Christ, who has blessed us in Christ with every spiritual blessing in the heavenly places, even as he chose us in him before the foundation of the world, that we should be holy and blameless before him. In love he

> predestined us for adoption through Jesus Christ, according to the purpose of his will, to the praise of his glorious grace, with which he has blessed us in the Beloved. In him we have redemption through his blood, the forgiveness of our trespasses, according to the riches of his grace, which he lavished upon us, in all wisdom and insight making known to us the mystery of his will, according to his purpose, which he set forth in Christ as a plan for the fullness of time, to unite all things in him, things in heaven and things on earth.
>
> In him we have obtained an inheritance, having been predestined according to the purpose of him who works all things according to the counsel of his will, so that we who were the first to hope in Christ might be to the praise of his glory. In him you also, when you heard the word of truth, the gospel of your salvation, and believed in him, were sealed with the promised Holy Spirit, who is the guarantee of our inheritance until we acquire possession of it, to the praise of his glory. (Ephesians 1:3-14)

The abundant life is real, and God wants you to have it, not because we have done anything at all deserving, but simply because He has chosen us out of love, adopting us who were orphans, giving us an inheritance - one which exists in this life and the next - one of a future and a hope.

The Promised Land

We only live in the tension of being in between promise and fulfillment because of the fact that there is a Promised Land, and we are not there yet. The Land of Promise stands in contrast to the Land of In Between. There will come a point in the existence (we hesitate to use the word time here, as it has no meaning in the Promised Land) of every Christian when all the promises God has made to them will be fulfilled. It has already happened, but is yet to be fully realized. In the fullness of His Kingdom rule, He will perform all that He has promised, and in doing so, keep covenant with His people. Commonly referred to as heaven, this presence of Kingdom fullness will eradicate the tension we now endure - as God will bring to completion the entirety of what He has promised. In that day, the fullness of the blessings of His Kingdom reign will be upon His people.

So it is that we live in the now of His Kingdom with an eye to the not yet of the Promised Land.

The balance of the books in this series will focus on assisting the reader in their walk in the Land of In Between, as they sojourn on the way to the Promised Land. Our goal is to help us all to be able to overcome, while living with the tension of yet-to-be fulfilled promises. The series will focus on the transformation that must take place within us to have such victory and enjoy the abundance of this life which Jesus intends for each of us to have. *This life is abundant* - full of everything He is.

May the Lord bless you, as you live abundantly in Him in the now, with your hope firmly set on the not yet!

References

Augustine, Saint. Confessions. Book 1. New York: Penguin Books, 1961.

Bonhoeffer, Dietrich. Life Together. San Francisco: Harper & Row Publishers, 1954. The Cost of Discipleship. New York: MacMillan Publishing Company, 1963. "Who Am I?" Letters and Papers From Prison. New York: MacMillan Publishing Company, 1953.

Bradshaw, John. Healing the Shame That Binds You. Deerfield Beach, Florida: Health Communications, Inc., 1988.

Brunner, Emil. Man in Revolt. Philadelphia: The Westminster Press, 1939.

Buechner, Frederick. Magnificent Defeat. San Francisco: Harper San Francisco Division of Harper Collins Publishers, 1966. The Clown in the Belfry. San Francisco: Harper San Francisco Division of Harper Collins Publishers, 1992. The Hungering Dark. New York: HarperCollins Publishers, 1969.

Chesterson, Gilbert K. "Gilbert K. Chesterson Quotes." Brainy Quote. BrainyMedia.com 2006. <http://brainyquotes.com/quotes/quotes/g/gilbertkc102389.html>.

Churchill, Winston. "Winston Churchill Quotes." Brainy Quote. BrainyMedia.com 2006. <http://www.brainyquote.com/quotes/quotes/w/winstonchu125060.html> & <http://www.brainyquote.com/quotes/quotes/w/winstonchu133395.html>.

Crabb, Larry. Foreword. Cry of the Soul. By Dr. Dan B. Allender and Dr. Tremper Longman III. Colorado Springs: NavPress, 1999. The Pressure's Off: There's a New Way to Live. Colorado Springs: WaterBrook Press, 2002. Understanding People. Grand Rapids: Zondervan, 1987.

Crowe, Sheryl. "Soak Up the Sun." C'mon C'mon. Interscope Records, B0000636UN, 2002.

Dana, H.E. & Mantey, Julius R. A Manual Grammar of the Greek New Testament. Toronto, Canada: 1927

Eldredge, John. Waking the Dead. Nashville: Thomas Nelson Publishers, 2003.

Fenelon, Francois de Salignac de. Let Go. Whitaker Distributors, 1973.

Forrest Gump. Director Robert Zemeckis. Paramount Pictures, 1994.

Franken, Al. Lies and the Lying Liars Who Tell Them: A Fair and Balanced Look at the Right. New York: Penguin Group, 2004.

Furnish, Victor Paul. 2 Corinthians, Anchor Bible, New York: Doubleday, 1984.

Gelman, David & Friday, Carolyn. "Overstressed by Success." Newsweek June 3, 1991: 56.

Hayford, Jack. Live Teaching. International Church of the Foursquare Gospel. Date Unknown.

Johnston, Tom & Perkinson, Mike Chong. A New Testament Trilogy: Our God, Ourselves, Our Community. St. Charles: ChurchSmart Resources, 2005.

Koyama, Kosuke. Three Mile An Hour God. Maryknoll, NY: Orbis Books, 1980.

Kreig, Charles. "Expecting the Worst." Pastor's Story File. Ed. James S. Hewett. April 1988. 1.

Lewis, C.S. The Chronicles of Narnia: The Lion, The Witch, and the Wardrobe. New York: Macmillan, 1953. The Chronicles of Narnia: The Silver Chair. New York: Macmillan, 1953.

Lovelace, Richard F. Dynamics of Spiritual Life: An Evangelical Theology of Renewal. Downers Grove, Ill.: InterVarsity Press, 1979.

Lloyd-Jones, D. Martyn. Studies on the Sermon on the Mount. Grand Rapids, Michigan: WM. B. Eerdmans Publishing Company, 1959.

Lucado, Max. On the Anvil. Carol Stream: Tyndale House Publishers, Inc., 1985.

Manning, Brennan. Ruthless Trust: The Ragamuffin's Path to God. San Francisco: HarperCollins, 2000.

Martin, Ralph. 2 Corinthians, Word Biblical Commentary. Waco, Texas: Word Books, 1986.

Martindale, Wayne & Root, Jerry. The Quotable Lewis. Wheaton, Illinois: Tyndale House Publishers, Inc., 1989.

McCord, David. "Quotes by David McCord." Zaadz Pre-Beta. Zaadz, Inc. 2006. <http://www.zaadz.com/quotes/David_McCord>.

Miller, Donald. Searching for God Knows What. Nashville: Nelson Books, 2004.

Miller, Keith. A Second Touch. Word Books, 1972.

Murphy-O'Connor, Jerome. Becoming Human Together: The Pastoral Anthropology of St. Paul. Wilmington: Michael Glazier, Inc., 1982.

Naisbitt, David & Aburdene, Patricia. Mega Trends 2000. New York: William Morrow and Company, Inc., 1990.

Overman, Steve. Private Conversation. October 1990.

Packer, J. I. Knowing God. Downers Grove: InterVarsity Press, 1975.

Peck, Scott. The Road Less Traveled. New York: Simon & Schuster, 1978.

Pennington, M. Basil. "The Call to Contemplation." Weavings. May/June 1996: 35.

Redmond, Matt. "Blessed Be Your Name." Where Angels Fear to Tread. Sparrow, 2005.

Reynolds, David. Playing Ball on Running Water. San Francisco: HarperCollins, 1984.

Terminator 2: Judgement Day. Dir. James Cameron. TriStar Pictures, 1991.

"The Eye of the Beholder." The Twilight Zone. Writ. by Rod Sterling and dir. by Douglas Heyes. CBS TV Network. Season 2, Episode 42. 1960-1961.

"The Place of Acceptance." Discipleship Journal. Issue Sixty, 1990: 16.

The Wizard of Oz. Dir. Victor Fleming. Warner Brothers, 1939.

Tozer, A. W. That Incredible Christian. Harrisburg: Christian Publications, 1964.

U2. "I Still Haven't Found What I'm Looking For." The Joshua Tree. Island Records, Inc, 422 842 298-2, 1987.

Van Dyke, Henry. "Quotation #22305 from Rand Lindsly's Quotations." The Quotations Page. 1994-2006. <http://www.quotationspage.com/quote/22305.html>.

Willard, Dallas. "Looking Like Jesus." Christianity Today. 20 August 1990: 29-31.

Willy Wonka and the Chocolate Factory. Director Mel Stuart. Warner Home Video, 1971.